TONY EVANS

CALLED

for a

PURPOSE

HARVEST HOUSE PUBLISHERS
EUGENE, OREGON

Scripture quotations are taken from the New American Standard Bible®, © 1960, 1962, 1963, 1968, 1971, 1972, 1973, 1975, 1977, 1995 by The Lockman Foundation. Used by permission. (www. Lockman.org)

Italicized emphasis in Scripture quotations is added by the author.

Cover design by Brian Bobel Design

Front cover photo © Oleg Breslavtsen / iStockphoto

Some material previously published in *Discover Your Destiny*.

From Tony Evans: I would like to thank my friends at Harvest House Publishers for their partnership in publishing. I would also like to thank Heather Hair for her skills and insights in collaborating on this manuscript.

Called for a Purpose

Copyright © by 2018 Tony Evans
Published by Harvest House Publishers
Eugene, Oregon 97408
www.harvesthousepublishers.com

ISBN 978-0-7369-6439-5 (hardcopy)
ISBN 978-0-7369-6440-1 (eBook)

Library of Congress Cataloging-in-Publication Data
Names: Evans, Tony, 1949- author.
Title: Called for a purpose / Tony Evans.
Description: Eugene : Harvest House Publishers, 2018.
Identifiers: LCCN 2018011249 (print) | LCCN 2018022034 (ebook) | ISBN
    9780736964401 (ebook) | ISBN 9780736964395 (pbk.)
Subjects: LCSH: Vocation--Christianity.
Classification: LCC BV4740 (ebook) | LCC BV4740 .E93 2018 (print) | DDC
    248.4--dc23
LC record available at https://lccn.loc.gov/2018011249

Printed in the United States of America

18 19 20 21 22 23 24 25 26 / VP-GL / 10 9 8 7 6 5 4 3 2

A Savory Life

We know that God causes all things to work together for good to those
who love God, to those who are called according to His purpose.

Romans 8:28

Have you ever felt a little hungry, opened up the refrigerator, and thought to yourself, "Hmm...what to eat? I know—a stick of butter! Yeah, that sounds great."

Probably not. A large serving of butter doesn't taste very good all by itself. Neither does flour. Or salt, or baking soda. Or most cooking ingredients, actually. Yet a master chef gathers them all together, blending them to accomplish her intended purpose. Then she puts them in the oven, and the scent of a freshly baked cake lures everyone nearby into the kitchen.

In the same way, God can use the ingredients of our lives to accomplish His purpose. We often hear Romans 8:28 quoted: "We know that God causes all things to work together for good to those who love God, to those who are called according to His purpose."

However, people often refer only to one part of the verse: "All things work together for good." The problem is that all things *do not* work together for good. To quote only half the verse is to miss the whole meaning. The promise is to people who love God and are called according to His purpose.

God has a purpose for you, and the first step in discovering your purpose is to surrender to that truth.

Only when you are living your life according to His purpose, not your own, will He cause all things to blend together for your good and His glory. Otherwise, the "all things" may still happen to you, but they won't necessarily be carefully mixed together to accomplish God's good purpose in your life.

Today, if your life is like a stick of butter or a cup of flour or a few tablespoons of salt, take the first step to turn it into something savory by surrendering to God's will and seeking His purpose for you. When you are committed to Him above all else, He will mix all things in your life—the good, the bad, and the bitter—and turn them into something divine.

Lord, open my eyes to see Your purpose in my life. Help me to surrender everything to You, and reveal to me the goodness that comes when You merge my life experiences together to bring me to my destiny.

Preparing for the Good Stuff

The LORD will accomplish what concerns me;
Your lovingkindness, O LORD, is everlasting;
Do not forsake the works of Your hands.

PSALM 138:8

Preparing for your calling is like going to a fine pizzeria, where skilled chefs start with a ball of dough. They roll the dough, pressing and mashing it. Then they start pounding on it. After banging it around for a while, they start throwing it up in the air and twirling it. That dough goes through a whole lot so that you and I can have the pleasure of eating it.

But when you go to a pizzeria, you don't ask for dough. You want the good stuff. You want the sauce, the cheese, and maybe some meat or veggies on top. Everyone wants the good stuff, but you can't get the good stuff until the dough has been prepared. In the same way, we have to be prepared for our calling. Sometimes our preparation starts with some pressing and some mashing. Sometimes we feel tossed around or banged up for a little while. But this is only in preparation for the good stuff.

Throughout life's bumps and bruises, God is preparing you for the perfect destiny He has created you to live out. Yet your response to those bumps and bruises may determine how quickly you reach your destiny. It's easy to throw in the towel and walk away when life's challenges seem pointless or too painful. But if you will keep your eyes focused on God's purpose for you, not your pain, God will use your trials for your good and His glory. He works all things together for good when you love Him and live according to your calling. No pain or experience is wasted when you are a child of the King.

Keep your eyes focused on the destination—the end result—and you will find the strength for the journey that takes you there. You have a glorious destiny to discover and live out.

....

Father in heaven, in those moments (or hours or even years) of preparation, remind me that You have a good plan and purpose for my life. Give me the grace to trust You in it all so I do not waste time relearning the same lessons I need to know in order to fulfill my destiny.

Little Steps, Big Blessings

I urge you, brethren, by the mercies of God, to present
your bodies a living and holy sacrifice, acceptable to
God, which is your spiritual service of worship.

ROMANS 12:1

God will always test you for the big things by looking at the little things. I knew at 18 years old that God wanted me to preach. But I started out on street corners and bus stops, not in churches. I would stand in front of bus stops where people were waiting for buses, and I'd go at it. I would instantly have a captive audience of 10 to 20 people.

There was no pay involved. There was no fame involved. In fact, I looked rather strange sometimes pacing back and forth on street corners preaching in (what some people call) my *loud* voice. But I was doing what God wanted me to do.

The church came later.

One day, my street-corner sermon led to a moment of decision. A very angry-looking man stood across from me. As I continued to preach, he approached me, placed his hand inside his front coat pocket, and said, "If you keep preaching, I'm going to shoot you." He glared at me with a hatred I'd never seen before.

I knew that preaching was my calling, but I began to question whether a busy street corner in Atlanta in the late 1960s was the right location. At the same time, I prayed, "Lord, I believe You have called me here to preach. I also believe that You heard my prayer for protection, and that You will keep me safe. Yet, Lord, if I perish, I will perish doing Your will."

Just as I finished the prayer, I was filled with an overwhelming confidence, and I continued my preaching with even more passion and volume. The man who had threatened me became more irritated and glared at me, but he eventually walked away.

Many of us are waiting for big blessings, but are we willing to be obedient in the small things? God has since granted me a large church and a national platform, but those didn't come without years of obedience as I took the steps He asked me to take. If God can't get you to do little acts of good works, why should He entrust you with even greater opportunities?

Always be faithful in the small things. God is watching, and He will reward your obedience to Him.

....

Dear God, I want to be faithful to You in the little things. I want to honor You in all that I do. Show me where and how You want me to take steps toward my destiny every day. Help me to remember that You are leading me on the perfect path to my purpose.

Custom-Made

I will cry to God Most High,
To God who accomplishes all things for me.

PSALM 57:2

My initials are sewn onto the cuff of several of my shirts. No one questions who owns those shirts because my initials—A.T.E.—demonstrate they are mine. I monogram the cuffs on the shirts that are tailored for me.

I also have other shirts that were bought off the rack. Many people could say they have shirts just like them, and those people would be right. But they wouldn't be able to say that about the shirts with my initials sewn in because those shirts were custom-made.

When a garment is custom-made, it's fitted to your unique shape. It is crafted with you in mind. That means it's not for anyone else to wear.

We are all unique. We are all custom-made. We have no reason to try to be someone else or to live someone else's life. Why settle for off-the-rack living when there is an identity and destiny custom-made for you? When you are living out your destiny, you aren't measuring who you are by comparing yourself to someone else. You aren't measured by what you have done according to what someone else has done. Rather, when you are living out your destiny, you measure what you have done according to what God created you to do.

Yet many people spend much of their lives trying to be somebody else. Why try to be somebody else? God already has one of them. There is only one you—and you are it. One of the first steps to living out your destiny is to realize it's *your* destiny. God made you unique on purpose because He has a plan that only your personality, background, temperament, mindset, and skills can fulfill. Embrace who you are—stop the comparisons. Halt the competitions. Let go of the jealousy, envy, or regret. Be the *you* God made you to be, and you will be on your way to manifesting the purpose God has created you to fulfill.

Lord, help me to embrace my uniqueness. Reveal to me the special attributes that only I have, and show me how You can use them in a grand way as You lead me in my destiny. Help me not to complain about my differences, but to thank You for them.

God's Masterpiece

*We are His workmanship, created in Christ Jesus for good works,
which God prepared beforehand so that we would walk in them.*

The great Italian sculptor, painter, architect, and poet Michelangelo once said, "In every block of marble I see a statue as plain as though it stood before me, shaped and perfect in attitude and action. I have only to hew away the rough walls that imprison the lovely apparition to reveal it to the other eyes as mine see it."

In an imperfect, jagged-edged, bulky, and unshaped block of marble, Michelangelo saw the treasure within. He once described the process this way: "I saw the angel in the marble and carved until I set him free." He could do this because Michelangelo didn't see what the marble was; he saw what the marble would be.

He saw a masterpiece.

This is similar to how God sees you on every step of the path to your destiny. You are a masterpiece. We read about this in the book of Ephesians: "We are His workmanship, created in Christ Jesus for good works, which God prepared beforehand so that we would walk in them."

This verse is referring to you, me, and all other children of God. The Greek word translated "workmanship" in this verse is *poiēma*, from where we also get our English word "poem." This word denotes a work of art or a masterpiece. You have been made as a work of God. You are His *poiēma*. You weren't created on the assembly line or as a random object thrown together to fill up space or time. When God made you, He went to work intentionally and delicately crafting your personality, looks, passions, and skills, even allowing your imperfections. God planted all His dreams for you into one magnificent work of art.

You are His masterpiece. You are God's handiwork. What's more, you were made with a purpose. And that purpose includes more than merely showcasing your talents. It involves influencing your world for good by fulfilling your destiny in all the places and ways God has positioned you to do so.

....

Father, thank You for making me a masterpiece. I know I can do all things through Christ who strengthens me. With Your powerful presence in my life, I am able to live out my destiny to its fullest. Thank You for the wonderful plans You have in store for me, and may I be used as a blessing to influence others for good.

The Master of the Piece

Before I formed you in the womb I knew you,
And before you were born I consecrated you.

JEREMIAH 1:5

A number of characteristics make up a masterpiece. The first one is that a masterpiece is rare—like you. In order for something to be a masterpiece, it cannot exist all over the place.

Another characteristic about a masterpiece is that a masterpiece is special. Again, like you. In fact, you are so special that God sent His own Son to live for you, die for you, and rise from the dead for you so you can be all that you were intended to be.

A masterpiece is also valuable. If someone owns a masterpiece, they paid a large price for it. In fact, most masterpieces are carefully locked away in secure locations, such as museums and art galleries. That speaks volumes to the value of a masterpiece. I hope you know that it also speaks volumes about you.

A fourth characteristic of a masterpiece is that it is named by its creator. The artist or sculptor ascribes a name to his or her creation that reflects its meaning and purpose. You also have a name. It is your purpose. Your name encompasses the divine reason for your existence.

God not only named you but also knows you. A masterpiece is associated with its creator. We listen to Handel's *Messiah* or Beethoven's Fifth Symphony. We look at Michelangelo's *David* or Monet's

Sunflowers. A masterpiece is rarely known simply by its own name but also by the one who made it—the *master* of the piece. As a child of God, you are uniquely created by Him. He has made you and desires to be connected to you. He also wants others to know you in connection with Him. He wants those who see you to say, "I know her," or "I know him"; "That's God's Sarah," or "That's God's Matt," or "That's God's _____. " (Fill in your name—you are known.)

As a masterpiece, you are rare, special, valuable, named, and known in connection with your Creator. Think of yourself that way. Embrace yourself that way. Honor yourself that way. In so doing, you are honoring the One who made you.

....

Gracious God, thank You for making me rare, special, valuable, named, and known. Thank You that in all these things I find my purpose and security. You are a great and loving God, and I praise You for being so intentional about creating me.

The Blueprint

I glorified You on the earth, having accomplished
the work which You have given Me to do.

JOHN 17:4

The Westminster Shorter Catechism begins by addressing a foundational need in all of us—to identify why we are here. The question is asked, "What is the chief end of man?" The answer: "Man's chief end is to glorify God, and to enjoy Him forever." How do you glorify God? One way is by fulfilling His intended purpose for your life.

We read in the Gospel of John that Jesus acknowledged this. "I glorified You on the earth, having accomplished the work which You have given Me to do." How did Jesus glorify God? By completing the work God sent Him to do. The same is true for you. You bring glory to God as you walk in and fulfill His intended purpose for your life. You glorify God when you choose to live out your destiny—intentionally pursuing the works God has prepared for your life.

When you consider fulfilling your destiny, you can breathe a sigh of relief. Why? Because you don't have to carry the weight of creating it. No statue, painting, or song ever bore the burden of creating itself. God has already determined the destiny for your life. Your job is to walk in it. You were "created in Christ Jesus for good works, *which God prepared beforehand*" (Ephesians 2:10).

God already knows the end from the beginning. He has prepared your destiny beforehand.

> Remember this, and be assured…
> Remember the former things long past,
> For I am God, and there is no other;
> I am God, and there is no one like Me,
> *Declaring the end from the beginning,*
> And from ancient times things which have not been done,
> Saying, "My purpose will be established,
> and I will accomplish all My good pleasure" (Isaiah 46:8-10).

God works in much the same way that a carpenter works to build a house. A carpenter doesn't start nailing pieces of wood together and hope that he eventually comes up with a house. No, first a design is created, showing what the house is supposed to look like. Measurements are determined, along with a plan for placing critical components, such as electricity, plumbing, and heating. Only when the carpenter can see the finished work on his blueprint does he begin digging the foundation and ordering the materials.

When God says He declares the end from the beginning, He is saying He has already completed the blueprint in the spiritual realm for what you are to do in the physical realm. He knows your destiny. His goals for you are already made. His desires for you have already been determined. He has already dreamed His dream for you. Now He is simply rolling back through time to look for your cooperation as you begin walking in what He has already prepared for you to do.

....

Lord, strengthen me to walk in all that You have already prepared. Show me which way to go and guide me with Your wisdom along the way.

Our Power Source

I am the vine, you are the branches; he who abides in Me and I in him, he bears much fruit, for apart from Me you can do nothing.

JOHN 15:5

Sometimes Christians look at other Christians and say, "I wish I could be as spiritual as they are," or "I wish I could do something as exciting and important as they do." But every believer needs to understand that we all find our identity in Christ and we all have the same source—God.

So if someone seems to be progressing in their spiritual walk faster than you, they may be living in light of who they are while you are not. They may be tapping into God, our source, on a more regular basis through ongoing thoughts of surrender and gratitude.

In my kitchen, I have a toaster, a can opener, a microwave, and a refrigerator. They are all different appliances, but they work from the same power source. When I plug them in, the can opener opens the cans, the refrigerator keeps food cold, the microwave heats it, and the toaster toasts it. Each appliance is different, but it lives up to its manufactured specifications because each appliance is receiving power from the same source.

Even though I am different from you and you are different from me, all of us have the same potential to live up to God's ideal for us. You can be what God created you to be, and I can be what God created me to be because the same power current is available to all of us in the body of Christ. It's available to all who belong to God.

God has the perfect destiny for you, but you must know who you are in Him and tap into His wisdom and power through an ongoing abiding relationship with Him.

Lord, make my life a living testimony of Your power flowing through me. I understand that this means I need to make abiding with You a priority in my life. When I get busy, remind me to slow down and meditate on Your presence. Show me ways I can abide with You throughout my day, whether that be through listening to songs that glorify You, reading Your Word, thinking about You, or communicating with You about everything. Increase my awareness of You, Lord, so I can abide more.

The Highways of Life

Things which eye has not seen and ear has not heard, and
which have not entered the heart of man, all that
God has prepared for those who love Him.

1 CORINTHIANS 2:9

A boxcar on a train has no power to move down the tracks on its own. It isn't going anywhere unless it's hooked up. Your life as a Christian is like a boxcar on a train. It is designed to be hooked up to the engine of God's purpose. If your life is not hooked up to the purpose for which God has you here, you are not going anywhere. You are stuck.

But what is worse—to be stuck, or to feel lost? Sometimes on the way to your destiny, you may feel like you are going around in circles and getting nowhere.

"Mixmaster" is the name of some "stack interchanges," where a series of highways intersect. Most Mixmasters are near the downtown area of a city. At the point where the highways connect, you will find their purpose. In your life there are also highways that lead to the center of your purpose. The highways of experience, opportunities, passions, and abilities are all designed to lead you to the intersection of your purpose in God and your calling for your life here on earth. Where these four things intersect—experience, opportunities, passions, and abilities—your purpose starts.

As you journey the path toward your destiny, remember to always stay hooked up to the engine of God so He can take you where you need to go. And don't despair when it seems that you are on roads going nowhere. You will discover in time, when you reach the Mixmaster of your life, that these roads will eventually meet at the point of your purpose. Keep going—taking one day at a time—knowing in the end, all roads lead to your destiny when you love God and are called according to His will for you.

Almighty God, sometimes the roads of my life don't seem to lead me to my destiny. But You know better. You are working behind the scenes either preparing me, or preparing those I will one day connect with, to fulfill what You have planned. Encourage my spirit when I cannot see the end result—encourage me to keep going in faith knowing You have a perfect destination in store.

The Play-Action Pass

Satan disguises himself as an angel of light.

2 Corinthians 11:14

Do you like to watch football? I do. I loved it as a kid, I loved watching my son play in high school and in college and even a bit in the NFL, and I love to watch it now after a long Sunday morning of back-to-back services at church. Watching football is never dull to me.

One play that often works well is called a play-action pass. The quarterback receives the ball from the center, turns as if he is about to hand the ball off to the running back…but then keeps the ball. The goal of the fake is to get the defense to focus on the running back—until they realize he doesn't even have the ball. While this is going on, the quarterback quickly hides the ball, runs the other way, and throws a pass to a receiver downfield.

If the quarterback has done his job well, the defense has been lured away from the ball, and the quarterback can throw it to a wide-open receiver.

So why am I spending today's devotional talking to you about football? Because a preacher can get a lot of life illustrations from football! And this play is no different.

Satan has run a play-action pass on many of us today. He has lured us into running the wrong direction and chasing the wrong goals so he can distract us from our real purpose. Like a pickpocket who loves a crowd, Satan has been robbing too many people of their purpose by distracting them from God's plan.

One of the best strategies against the play-action pass is to be aware of its existence. When you are aware, your eyes will be open, and you will keep a greater focus on the ball rather than the fake. As you pursue your destiny, be aware of Satan's schemes so that if you feel you have become distracted from God's purpose for you, you can double back and get on track sooner rather than later.

Lord, open my eyes to see where Satan is seeking to deceive me. Help me to discern Your truth from his lies so I can pursue the purpose You have for me in all I do.

The Fire of Life's Passion

If I say, "I will not remember Him
Or speak anymore in His name,"
Then in my heart it becomes like a burning fire
Shut up in my bones;
And I am weary of holding it in,
And I cannot endure it.

JEREMIAH 20:9

The space shuttle is an enormous flying machine created to carry out a unique mission. It has been designed to go somewhere. Yet because of gravity, the space shuttle can't go anywhere by itself. It must be placed on a rocket and wheeled to the launch pad.

Before it gets to the launch pad, gravity tells it, "You aren't going anywhere. You are grounded." And gravity is right. But when it is on the launch pad and a fire is lit beneath it, this earthbound, multi-ton vehicle is able to soar.

Many of us are like a space shuttle sitting in a hangar—grounded—because of our fears. We are unable to live out our destiny because of things we have been told. We have poor self-esteem, and even though we desire to feel the surge of power beneath us, we sometimes think God is unable to create enough fire to lift this mess off the ground. Yet if fire can lift the space shuttle all the way out of the earth's atmosphere, fire can do the same for you too. Things move because of fire.

Your passion is your fire. What is that thing, subject, interest, or vision that stirs you up inside when you think about it? Whatever that is, when you connect that passion with an eternal perspective, you'll light a fire within.

Keep in mind that your purpose and your passion have eternal value written in them if they are aligned with the destiny given to you by God. So the question you need to ask yourself is this: What am I passionate about that is connected to eternity?

Scripture frequently says that God "stirred" the heart of a person He was calling to do something. How has God stirred your heart? What brings out your emotions? What breaks your heart or inspires and invigorates you? What do you do or even think about that makes you feel alive? If eternity is connected to it, that passion reveals your destiny. Pursue it. Chase it. Run after it. Go get it. Embrace it. Live it. Because without it, you will merely be existing—you won't be fulfilling your destiny.

If you're wondering what your passion is, a great question to ask is this: What would you do if money, family, or time was not an issue? What would that be? Do you have a secret ambition? If it is tied to eternity, then that is your passion. And unless you pursue your passion, your emotional life will wither and die. Passion left unaddressed dies or at least remains dormant.

．．．

God, please reveal and confirm to me my passion that is connected with my eternal purpose. Light the fire within me that will propel me to do that which You have created me to do.

Sneakers

Since we have so great a cloud of witnesses surrounding us, let us also lay aside every encumbrance and the sin which so easily entangles us, and let us run with endurance the race that is set before us.

HEBREWS 12:1

When I grew up, I often wore tennis shoes. They were also called sneakers back then, and like other kids, I used one pair for everything. I played basketball in them, went to school in them, and ran in them. Whatever I did, I did with my sneakers. They were made by Converse or Adidas or Reebok...and then Nike came along. Today people buy designer tennis shoes that cost an arm and a leg. On top of that, we now have a different kind of tennis shoe for every sport. You can't just run and walk in the same shoe; you have to have a different kind of shoe for each activity.

Why are running shoes different from walking shoes? The reason is that each shoe is specialized and crafted to fulfill a specific purpose.

In the same way, God has crafted every single believer according to where He wants you to take Him and to carry out His purposes. He crafted you with a specific reason in mind. He has a plan for you to be a part of—a plan that is bigger than you but includes you. It is broader than you, but you are an essential piece in carrying it out. God is the master planner and has constructed each of us in such a way that when He merges our destinies together, He accomplishes His overarching goal—advancing His kingdom on earth—in the most effective manner.

You aren't just any ordinary tennis shoe. You are special, uniquely designed on purpose and for a purpose. Live out your purpose, hone your skills, focus your attention, and accomplish all that God has in store for you.

....

Father, help me to run the race set before me according to where You want me to go. Show me the steps to take and the path to follow, and cause me to embrace the unique qualities You have built into me.

Motivation in the Mundane

The vision is yet for the appointed time;
It hastens toward the goal and it will not fail.
Though it tarries, wait for it;
For it will certainly come, it will not delay.

HABAKKUK 2:3

One of the reasons so many of us are unfulfilled is that we are driving in the wrong lane. We operate in lanes of life that were never intended for us. We operate in purposes that were never designed for us. All exits are good exits, but not all exits are your exits. We don't get off at an exit for no good reason when we are driving. We decide to get off at an exit because it will take us to our intended destination. We take the exit that will lead us to where we are supposed to go. Many people miss their purpose because they take any old exit that comes along. We should only take an exit that takes us toward our destiny, our purpose, or our calling. And one of the ways to know which exit to take is to combine our vision with our passion.

If there is something on your heart that burdens you or evokes strong emotions, before you try to talk yourself out of it or to rationalize it, ask God if this is a clue to your vision and your destiny. Most likely it is. Passion and vision are two things God gives you in order to motivate you for a sustained calling.

Once you jump into your purpose and start on the path toward your destiny, you will discover that every day is not a skip down the yellow brick road. Each hour doesn't come with fireworks and rainbows or exciting adventures to explore and conquer.

Along anyone's path to their destiny, there will be many dull moments and a lot of plain hard work. Passion and vision are gifts from God to strengthen you and motivate you through those times. They are critical to you fulfilling your destiny because they are the breath, or the wind, that gives you wings to soar and strength to keep going in the midst of the tedious and the mundane.

Living a life of destiny doesn't mean that every moment will be filled with bells and trumpets. It means that your passion and your vision will often have to carry you through the important but not-so-exciting activities so that you will arrive at your intended destination.

....

Father, I want to honor You with all that I do, even the things in my life that seem boring and mundane. Help me to be motivated to do these things by connecting them to my purpose, my destiny, and the vision You have given to me.

The Magic Pen

We walk by faith, not by sight.

2 Corinthians 5:7

Have you ever seen a child coloring in an invisible coloring book? The pictures in these coloring books are hidden until the child uses a "magic pen" to color over the blank paper. That's when an elaborate picture begins to appear.

This is similar to what happens with your vision. Before the beginning of time, God established your purpose and your destiny. The image of what you will become and what you have been designed to do may be hidden from you right now, but it has already been established. Every line, shape, and color is already there. But you won't get to see it or experience it until you take the "magic pen" of faith and do what God has revealed to you to do.

Like a child looking at an uninteresting coloring book of blank pages, you may start coloring in faith hesitantly. Yet as you begin to see God respond to your movements by revealing more and more of His vision for you, you will be motivated to continue on in faith.

As God reveals your vision to you, your best move is to act on whatever He shows you. Take a step in the little that He has shown you, because God loves to hit a moving target. As you step out a little, He will show you much. As you step out again, He will show you even more. As you step out even more, He will show you the most you can receive. But unless you respond to the little, you will never discover the most. That's why Paul calls it "walking by faith." It involves doing something; it involves movement.

So take up your magic pen of faith and start coloring your life. You'll be amazed at the beautiful design that will begin to emerge.

....

Dear God, as I walk through this maze of life, I can't always see what's around the corner. I am not always assured that I will know what to expect after I take my next step. That's why I need You to strengthen my faith in small ways so that I can learn to step out in even bigger ways. Will You give me greater faith as I exercise my faith muscles every day? Please guide me in ways that this can be done.

First Things First

Seek first His kingdom and His righteousness,
and all these things will be added to you.

MATTHEW 6:33

One day, a man who had two cows told his wife they should sell them. He and his wife could keep the money from one cow, and they could give the money from the other cow to God.

But the next day, the man walked into his house looking sad. "What's wrong?" his wife asked.

The man thought for a minute and then replied, "God's cow just died."

When you seek first your own dreams, your desires, your plans, your programs, your agenda...God's cow is always the one that dies. He always gets what's left over. The first thing to suffer is time with Him, obedience to Him, or commitment to His plans. And yet at the same time, you may still pray, "Dear God, bless my rule, my reign, my plan." Yet God is not going to bless any plan but His.

The secret to living out the fullness of your destiny is found in one word: "first." It represents your highest priority—to advance the rule of God and His kingdom in every area of your life. We read this word in Matthew 6:33: "Seek first His kingdom and His righteousness, and all these things will be added to you." There is a hierarchy in God's kingdom, and He is always first.

You can listen to a million sermons, read a million books, and pray a million prayers over a million years, but none of those things will empower you to live out your destiny until you put God first. God must be first.

In baseball, if you miss first base, it doesn't matter whatever else you do after that. If you miss first base but go on to touch second base, third base, and home plate—and even if everyone congratulates you when you get there—you are still out. If you miss what is first, it doesn't matter what else you do.

Change one thing in your life, and you will get to watch that one thing change everything else. From this point forward, put God *first* in all of your life. Not because it is His request, but because it is His demand. God promises that when you do, "all these things will be added to you." You will experience the fullness and maximum potential of who you are along with the blessings He has in store for you as you enter into what He has ordained you to be.

....

Great God and King, I put You first in my heart, my mind, my schedule, and all that I do. I make this commitment to You today to go to You first in the decisions I make, to read Your Word, and to seek Your wisdom. Thank You for that which You have promised me when I make You first in my life.

God's Warranty

David, after he had served the purpose of God in his own generation,
fell asleep, and was laid among his fathers and underwent decay.

ACTS 13:36

People often have warranties on the major products they own in
their homes. A warranty simply guarantees that the manufacturer
will stand behind their product. It's a guarantee that if there's a defect
or a failure, the manufacturer will stand behind the product. But all
warranties have limitations.

The warranty is not designed to cover abuse by the owner. You can't
take your toaster, throw it against the wall, jump on it, or run it over,
and then claim the product warranty. Warranties are offered under
the assumption that the product will be used for its intended purpose.

God's got a warranty on your life as long as you're using it for His
purposes and existing for His glory. A great biblical example of this
is found in the life of King David. David was not a perfect man, but
Scripture calls him a man after God's own heart.

In the book of Acts, we discover what a man after God's own heart
is all about: "David, after he had *served the purpose of God* in his own
generation, fell asleep, and was laid among his fathers" (Acts 13:36).
David was about more than just church attendance, Bible reading
and memorization, committee membership, and dancing in the street.
David, a man after God's own heart, was a man after God's purpose.

David's biblical epitaph tells us a lot simply by what it does not say. We do not read, "David, after he had become the head of the company," or "David, after he had made so much money," or "David, after he had won so many battles," or "David, after he had risen in the social circles," or "David, after he had purchased a lot of brand-name clothes…"

No, instead it reads, "David, after he had served the purpose of God…" That's what it means to be a man or woman after God's own heart. David did what he had been put on earth to do. David knew that it wasn't about him and that God's blessings were tied to God's purpose. He realized that his destiny was tied to God's desires, and that the blessings he received flowed out of his destiny and were not independent of it.

....

God, grant me the wisdom to know my purpose and the self-control to pursue it rather than becoming distracted by other things vying for my attention. I know that You have my back and that You will cover me as I pursue the purpose You have for me. Thank You for that, Lord.

Seeing Through the Fog

"I know the plans that I have for you," declares the LORD, "plans for welfare and not for calamity to give you a future and a hope."

JEREMIAH 29:11

Florence Chadwick was the first woman to swim both directions of the English Channel. Early in her career, she attempted to swim the approximately 26 miles from Catalina Island to the California coast. On that day, the grueling swim was made even more difficult by a dense fog. After more than 15 hours in the icy water of the Pacific, Florence decided to quit. Unable to see her destination, she lost both the motivation and the strength to continue.

She waved to the boat that was trailing her to let her team know she wanted them to pick her up. When it neared, she climbed in, exhausted. After she got in, she was asked why she had quit. Florence replied that she gave up because she did not know how far she had to go since she could not see the land through the fog. Less than a mile from her destination, she quit simply because she lost hope in what she could not see.

Florence was a fierce competitor at heart and did not waste the defeat. Instead, she learned from it. Some months after giving up, Florence decided to swim from Catalina to California once again. On that day, the same thick fog covered the water, preventing her from seeing the nearing land. Having learned from her previous experience,

Florence determined not to give up. She later said she maintained a mental picture of the California shoreline the entire time she swam. With every stroke, she saw her destination. Because she had a vision of where she was going, she was finally able to get there.

What you see matters. Your vision of your future matters. Is it one of fear, disappointment, or doubt? Or do you see a future full of goodness and hope, like the one God says He has for you (Jeremiah 29:11)? Vision is a powerful mental tool that you should sharpen on a regular basis because it will give you the courage to continue even when life's fog prevents you from seeing what's ahead.

....

God, thank You for the powerful tool of vision and for helping me to persevere by looking to the promises found in Your Word.

Connected to the Source

Whoever drinks of the water that I will give him shall
never thirst; but the water that I will give him will become
in him a well of water springing up to eternal life.

JOHN 4:14

When I was growing up in Baltimore, the way we "swam" on Saturday was to run through the water from the fire hydrant. The fire marshal would come and open the fire hydrant enough for it to spray water for us. The fire hydrant would shoot out water; we'd put on our shorts and have the time of our lives.

As a young boy, I didn't understand how all that water could come out of that little pipe for days. Water just kept gushing out of there. When I asked my dad about it, he explained that the pipe in the hydrant had no water. The water all came from underneath the ground. The pipe from the hydrant connected with another pipe that led to a reservoir, and the reservoir had plenty of water.

My dad explained to me that as long as there was an underground connection, plenty of water would come out of the pipe. If nothing was coming out of the pipe, we didn't need to fix the pipe—we needed an underground connection.

In the same way, we all need something underneath that connects us with the source so that water can flow from our lives.

Many people struggle today to locate their destiny. They spend so much time looking for the plan, the purpose, and the calling, they forget where all of that originates. It originates in God Himself. If you can't find your destiny, don't go searching for it—go searching for God. Deepen your relationship with Him, spend time with Him…He's the connection you need because He's the One who already knows what you want to know. He knows your destiny, and as you connect with Him as your Source for all things, you will also tap into the full force of your purpose.

....

Lord God, You are the source of all that I need. With Your wisdom and guidance, I can fulfill the reason I was put here on earth. But to experience that, I need to draw closer in my connection to You. I ask that You will bless me as I seek to do just that.

Who Are You?

As many as received Him, to them He gave the right to become
children of God, even to those who believe in His name.

John 1:12

Many people today are running here and there, trying to find themselves. This search is meaningless. If you don't know who you are, how do you know what to look for? And how do you know when you have found you, since you don't know what you are looking for?

Toasters don't find themselves. Refrigerators don't find themselves. Appliances don't find themselves, because their purpose has been assigned by another. A toaster doesn't have to find its reason for being; it just does what the manufacturer made it to do.

As a Christian, you don't have to look for yourself. God has already given you a destiny—a divine reason for being. Your purpose is to fulfill it.

If you are not fulfilling His purpose in your life, you might watch more television, shop for more things, hang out with more friends, and try to get a better job, and yet your life will still feel empty because you are disconnected from God's purpose for your life. Not only that, but you won't feel valuable because you won't be satisfying your deep desire to fulfill your destiny. Without living out your destiny, you are settling for less than you are truly worth.

If a person walks around with a hundred dollars in her pocket but never uses it for what it was intended for, that hundred-dollar bill is just a piece of paper. It's valuable paper, but it's meaningless until utilized for its purchasing power. Similarly, God has assigned value to you. But until you live out your life for the purposes He intended, you will be trapped in a meaningless existence—holding on to intended value but not using it.

....

Lord, I recognize that You have placed great value in my life simply by my creation and calling. I don't want to waste the talents, ideas, love, and abilities You have given me. Give me wisdom to live my life to its fullest, truly manifesting every intended result You have destined for me.

The Value of Sand

He predestined us to adoption as sons through Jesus Christ
to Himself, according to the kind intention of His will.

EPHESIANS 1:5

Sand is cheap. In fact, at the beach, it's free. You can scoop up as much as you want, build a sand castle, bury yourself halfway, and no one is going to charge you a thing. After all, it's just sand, right?

Yet once sand is bagged to put it on a playground, it begins to increase in its value. You now have to pay something in order to use it. What used to be free on the beach now costs you several dollars for a 25-pound bag.

Go a step further and glue that sand to a piece of paper in order to make sandpaper, and its value per square inch has gone up even higher. Its value has increased because its purpose has been changed.

The major constituent of sand is silica. When it is heated and processed, it becomes an intricate part of a computer chip that could be worth thousands of dollars. So what was once free on the beach now has value because it is in a bag, because it is glued on a piece of paper, or because it is in a computer chip. The sand is the same, but it has found increased value in a greater purpose.

If you have not yet fully discovered your destiny, you may look around at your life and ask yourself what value there is in the things you are doing. They may be noble things, and they are probably responsible things, but when they are not tied to your eternal destiny, they have little long-term meaning. Pursue your destiny with passion and expediency because when you discover the eternal impact of your actions, you will sense that you have greater value than you realized.

You won't have changed, and perhaps even the nuts and bolts of what you are doing won't have changed, but when you consider the eternal impact of your actions, you become more aware of their value. This will inspire you to approach each day with a new zest and vigor because you know the true value of your life.

....

Loving heavenly Father, You have predestined me for a purpose that is even greater than myself. It involves an eternal impact that I am to make on the lives of those with whom I come into contact. Show me my true value. Help me to see myself as You see me and to discover the good works You have for me to accomplish.

A Lesson from the Bowling Alley

You formed my inward parts;
You wove me in my mother's womb.

PSALM 139:13

Sylvia has been my administrative assistant for decades, and for as far back as I can remember, she has loved to bowl. Faithful and committed to getting that ball down the lane to knock down those pins, Sylvia spends her weekends with friends bowling.

I have to admit that I didn't know much about bowling until I listened to Sylvia talk about her weekend outings. I've learned that a lot goes into the sport. One way to find out how serious someone is about bowling is to look at their bowling ball. Serious bowlers use custom-made balls. These are constructed to just the right weight and grip for the particular bowler. To have a custom-made bowling ball is to increase the possibility of an effective delivery so you can hit the mark.

God has constructed every member of His body in a customized way. He has uniquely crafted every one of us to hit the mark of His purpose and calling on our lives. We are not on an automated assembly line, put together with identical parts. We have been uniquely crafted for His purpose. You are, in fact, custom-made.

When God set about crafting you, He gave you all that you need to carry out the purpose He has destined for you. That includes your personality, likes and dislikes, temperament, eye color, interests, drive, intellect, and focus. God made sure you have everything you need, custom-made for the specialized calling He has for you.

Don't view your differences as disappointments. View them as the results of God's hand preparing you for your purpose. He has a reason for making you the way you are and giving you everything you have. Now it's up to you to seek His heart to discover that reason so you can put it all to good use.

. . . .

Dear God, thank You for customizing my life for my purpose. Thank You for giving me all that I need to carry out the plan You have for me. I am excited to fully live out Your dream for me.

Giddyap!

The thing I loved most about the Lone Ranger was his horse, Silver. I loved to see Silver rear up at the end of the program. He was a perfectly trained companion for the Lone Ranger.

Did you know Silver wasn't always like that? If you didn't see the first episode of the Lone Ranger, you can't appreciate Silver—or the Lone Ranger himself, for that matter. He started as just one of a whole group of rangers. One day his band of rangers was ambushed, and he was the "lone" survivor.

The Lone Ranger was left for dead, but he alone recovered. When he began to get his strength back, he heard in a canyon below him the sound of a horse—the horse that would come to be known as Silver. He saw the horse as a way to escape from his situation. The only problem was that the horse was a wild stallion.

The whole first episode was about the Lone Ranger gaining control of Silver. Silver would throw him off; the Lone Ranger would get back on, only to be thrown off again. The Lone Ranger rode Silver until the horse got the message that he was no longer in charge. When the Lone Ranger took over the reins of Silver's life, the horse could now do things he would never have been able to do on his own—because he was under the control of his master.

God wants to ride you and me so we can do stuff we could never do on our own. When the story of your life is written about how God rode you, what will He have accomplished? What will have happened in your life because you moved when God said "giddyap" and stopped when He said "whoa"? What will God accomplish in your life because you yielded to His purposes?

....

Lord, I humble myself before You so You can use me according to Your purposes. I want You to control the reins of my life so I will experience the best possible outcomes in all that I do—according to Your eternal purposes and goals.

Focus on the Ball

Know that the Lord Himself is God;
It is He who has made us, and not we ourselves;
We are His people and the sheep of His pasture.

Psalm 100:3

My wife and I have lived in the same house for more than 30 years. It's a modest home in an older neighborhood. But one of the highlights of our location is that we are situated just a stone's throw from a golf course. It's a beautiful course stretching as far as the eye can see.

Granted, I don't play golf—I don't have the time—but if I did, a walk through the course on the weekends would probably become a habit.

The story is told of a man who wanted to learn to play golf, so he took a trip to the driving range. The little white ball was really doing a number on him, embarrassing him as he tried to master the skill of hitting it just where he wanted it to go.

Six times in a row the newcomer swung and missed the ball. He finally thought to himself, "This game provides a lot of exercise, but I don't have any idea what to do with that white ball." He failed at the sport because he failed to focus on the ball.

Many of us are involved in endless activity, not hitting a thing, because we are not living with focus. We are busy and getting a lot of exercise moving through life, but our lives are not fulfilling the goals God has for us. God's goals for our lives are specific. He has a specific location and destiny where He wants us to go. You have not been placed on this earth to randomly go through it without intention. God is a God of intention. He is a God of plans. If you take just a moment to study nature and consider how everything is carefully tied together and perfectly timed, your awe of God and respect for Him will grow.

Human beings are no different. The Lord has plans for each of us, and when they intersect, they fulfill His greater overarching plan. Keep your eye on the goal—God's destiny for you—and you will accomplish more than you ever dreamed.

Lord, You made me with a specific destination in mind for my life. Show me the way. Put me on the right path. Confirm my steps that are in alignment with Your will—in every way.

God's Loudspeaker

*I have put My words in your mouth and have covered you
with the shadow of My hand, to establish the heavens, to
found the earth, and to say to Zion, "You are My people."*

ISAIAH 51:16

We are surrounded by radio waves. But without a radio, those waves don't do us a whole lot of good. The waves transport the signal, but we cannot sense their presence. We don't realize they are all around us—until something transforms them into sound waves. When that happens, we can suddenly hear what was there all along but we couldn't sense.

Our ears aren't designed to hear radio waves. We don't pick up that signal. The radio, however, has been designed to receive that signal and project the sound—talk shows, music, news, and so on. The radio helps us to take in what we otherwise would never hear.

So it is with our bodies. God designed our bodies to be vehicles through which He expresses His kingdom program for us and for the world. To put it another way, our humanity is God's conduit, God's loudspeaker for achieving His goal.

You are God's mouthpiece—a reflection of His own glory and intention on earth. Never take that lightly. You have been tasked with a great destiny: to communicate to the world the heart of God Himself. We each have our own part to play in this grand broadcast, and when we come together under God, we are able to make our voices heard to an even greater extent.

Remember, your purpose is not only about you. The Lord has given each of us a purpose, and when our purposes intersect, they carry out His plan for our good, for His glory, and for the advancement of His kingdom on earth.

....

I am your mouthpiece, Lord. I have been given the awesome privilege to declare Your goodness to those around me. Where there is anger, let me communicate Your love. Where there is confusion, let me bring Your clarity. Where there is doubt, let me demonstrate faith. Where there is fear, let me be a conduit of Your peace.

Created for Significance

I will give thanks to You,
for I am fearfully and wonderfully made;
Wonderful are Your works,
And my soul knows it very well.

PSALM 139:14

All of us struggle with unique issues or challenges in our lives. But one of the dominating issues that plague many of us today is a lack of fulfillment. Jesus tells us in John 10:10, "I came that they may have life, and have it abundantly." An abundant life is not void, or empty. It is life as it was meant to be lived. It is full and satisfying. It is filled with meaning.

The nagging inner emptiness that many people feel today reveals a lack of personal fulfillment. People often feel unfulfilled in their relationships, their careers, their spiritual lives, and in other ways.

A lack of fulfillment is tied to a lack of destiny. If you don't know your destiny or are not working toward it or living it out, you will not feel fulfilled. You will not be able to tap into the most authentic, genuine part of who you are. Anytime you have to rely on artificial happiness, energy, enthusiasm, passion, vision, and so on, you are not tapping into the rawest part of you. Nothing can replace you being the way you were created to be. Nothing can measure up to true authentic living according to your very own unique destiny. Everything else may satisfy for a moment or at the surface level, but it will not satisfy you deeply and abundantly within your very core—where true fulfillment lives.

Jesus offers you the abundant life. But to have that life, you need to connect with the eternal purpose He has for you. In Him and His will, you will discover true and lasting fulfillment.

A person should never truly be satisfied with what the world deems as success because success can never bring you significance. Fulfilling your destiny answers your deep, God-given need for significance. Live your destiny, and you will live a life of great significance.

....

Thank You, God, that You made me on purpose for a purpose. Thank You that I am not a random happening or chance occurrence. You have created me for a life of significance.

Maps

In all your ways acknowledge Him,
and He will make your paths straight.

PROVERBS 3:6

I have an app on my iPhone called Maps. I can type two locations in Maps, and it will instantly display a route for me to follow to get from one place to the other. However, if I opened up Maps and typed in "Current Location" for my starting point but nothing for the intended destination, the app would not give me a response when I pushed the button labeled "Route." Without a destination, the "Route" button cannot respond with directions. This is because Maps cannot provide me with a route if I do not tell it where I am planning to go.

If you do not know where you are headed, you cannot know the route to get there. Rather than going through life with an intended destination, you will bounce here or there like a ball in a pinball machine. You will be left trying this, that, and the other direction…hopeful that one option will lead somewhere good. Rather than taking the straightest path to your destiny, you will meander. And as you surely know, a lot of time can be wasted by meandering.

When we live without a clear sense of direction, we struggle to know which decisions are most important and how to make them. Life is filled with ambiguity. Should you take that job? Should you move there? Should you date that person or marry that one? Should you volunteer in that capacity? Should you spend your time in that manner?

Direction matters, and knowing your intended destination will help you know how to answer the questions that will arise on your journey. Without clear direction, life is hit-and-miss.

....

Father, I don't want to waste any more of my time meandering. I acknowledge You as my leader and my God. You are my guide, leading me on the path of my destiny. Show me the steps I am to take and help me to joyfully follow You each step of the way.

Unfinished Creations

Let your light shine before men in such a way that they may see
your good works, and glorify your Father who is in heaven.

MATTHEW 5:16

My wife, Lois, and I once visited a museum in Italy that housed many of Michelangelo's unfinished works—piece after piece of incomplete statues. Some of them showed only an arm. Others might just have a foot or a shoulder. Some were almost finished, and others had been barely begun.

As I walked through this museum looking at statue after statue of unfinished creations, I was reminded of heaven. Many of us are likely to get to heaven and stand before God one day without having fulfilled our purpose on earth. We will be like one of those unfinished statues I saw that day in Italy with just an arm showing, or just a leg, or only a shoulder. All because God was never allowed to chisel out His complete design in us.

Michelangelo's completed works of art are displayed prominently in the most elite locations around the world. But those that were left undone are in a somewhat obscure museum in Italy. These pieces never reached their potential level of significance. Without signif cance, they remained unnamed and, for the most part, unseen.

Never forget—you are significant! You matter. Your destin ters. God has a plan for you that affects not only you, but s others as well. Just as God blessed Abraham to be a blessing to the whole world, God's plan for you is designed to have a broad influence.

Maybe you don't feel significant because you would prefer to be another gender, another height, or another race. But God purposely made you the gender, race, and height you are. God has arranged or allowed all the experiences in your life—the good, the bad, and the bitter—to prepare you to fulfill your destiny. You are the gender you are for your destiny. You are the race you are for your destiny. You are the person you are for your destiny.

You are significant. Don't let the culture's definition of significance keep you from being chiseled into the magnificent art that you are. Who knows what unfinished work might have received even more acclaim than Michelangelo's *David* had it been completed? Who knows what statue remains imprisoned in a block of stone with its significance hidden from sight?

Who knows what masterpiece God is creating in you?

....

Dear Savior, I am significant. I matter. You have created me with a purpose and an intention. I have a destiny to fulfill and a calling to live out. Thank You, God, for giving me all of this and so much more!

Growth in Groves

Just as we have many members in one body and all the members
do not have the same function, so we, who are many, are one
body in Christ, and individually members one of another.

ROMANS 12:4-5

A long the California coastline live some of the largest organisms
in the world—redwood trees. Redwoods can grow to a height
of more than 300 feet and a circumference of 40 feet. They average
between 500 and 700 years old, but some have been around for 2,000
years! They are a magnificent sight. The trees grow only in groves, and
their roots intertwine underneath the ground. No intertwining, no
growth. No connectedness, no growth.

You have a destiny that is unique to you. However, as you pursue
your purpose, you must never forget that God created you to help fulfill His purpose for all His children. Your destiny is yours alone, but
it is not just about you. Nor is it to be carried out in isolation. In the
body of Christ, we connect with others who are pursuing the same
overarching goal—to advance God's kingdom on earth. We are to
complement each other rather than compete. We are to love rather
than resent.

Only when you align your purposes with God's kingdom agenda
will you fully manifest all that He has in store for your life. There is
no such thing as a Lone Ranger Christian. Each of us has a part to

play in this grand drama of the ages, and we carry that out best when we honor and respect others and synergize with them in God's kingdom plan.

....

Lord God, I am part of Your overarching plan. My part is important and special, but unless it is connected to the whole, I will not fulfill it. Help me to see how best to link up with Your body in what I do, with others who are connected to You as well.

You in God and God in You

He made from one man every nation of mankind to live on
all the face of the earth, having determined their appointed
times and the boundaries of their habitation.

Acts 17:26

A re you living out your destiny right now? If you feel that you aren't, the reason may be that your identity is defined by the flesh rather than by the new creation placed in you through Jesus Christ. In Acts chapter 17, Paul gives us an idea of how comprehensive this reality is.

> The God who made the world and all things in it, since He is Lord of heaven and earth, does not dwell in temples made with hands; nor is He served by human hands, as though He needed anything, since He Himself gives to all people life and breath and all things; and He made from one man every nation of mankind to live on all the face of the earth, having determined their appointed times and the boundaries of their habitation, that they would seek God, if perhaps they might grope for Him and find Him, though He is not far from each one of us; for in Him we live and move and exist (Acts 17:24-28).

God has determined your appointed times and boundaries. He has set your destiny in motion. He has created something new within you, and you can locate your destiny by connecting with Him. It is "in

Him" that you live and move and exist. Your true identity comes from abiding in God and fulfilling that which He has destined you to do. In other words, when you discover who He is, you will discover who you are. If you ignore who He is in you, then you will never fully discover who you are. As a result, you will live your life in trial and error as you attempt to somehow locate yourself.

You discover who you are when you discover who He is operating within you. You discover who you are when you recognize the new creation inside of you.

Lord, I want to fully discover who I am, and that comes from more completely knowing who You are. Help me to know You. Give me spiritual wisdom and insight into who You are. Make Your presence real in my life and guide my thoughts, words, and actions.

Who Will Foot the Bill?

My God will supply all your needs according
to His riches in glory in Christ Jesus.

PHILIPPIANS 4:19

God always provides for what He destines. If you are not experiencing His provision, it could be that you are not walking in your destiny. God is not obligated to provide for the destiny you want to have; He is only obligated to provide for the destiny He has designed you to fulfill.

When Jonah boarded a ship to attempt to run from God to Tarshish—in the opposite direction of his purpose in Nineveh—we read that Jonah had to pay his own fare. Jonah had to foot his own bill. He had to cover himself. Such is the case when we venture into a direction that is not within God's purpose for our lives.

Elijah is a perfect example of someone who took God at His Word and trusted in His ability to provide for the calling He had given. One day God provided for Elijah with ravens. Another time He provided through a widow at Zarephath. Even though the source through which God provided varied from time to time, Elijah was faithful to do what God had purposed, knowing that God would provide for him along the way.

God will provide everything you need—financially, emotionally, and spiritually—to fulfill His purpose for you. Keep your eyes open for His provision, though, because it doesn't always come in the expected and ordinary ways. He will provide for you in a way that will allow you the greatest opportunity to maximize your destiny.

Thank You, God, for Your provision in my life. Thank You for meeting my emotional, spiritual, and financial needs. And where I may have needs, guide me into the abundance You have for me through Your promises of provision.

Uptown for a Reason

Who knows whether you have not attained royalty for such a time as this?

ESTHER 4:14

The biblical story of Esther is about a beautiful woman. God used Esther's beauty and her background to fulfill His destiny for her life. Because of her beauty, Esther was chosen by King Ahasuerus as his new bride. Yet once she moved into the big house and got used to the luxurious lifestyle, a plot was made for the genocide of her people. Apparently Esther had gotten so used to her new way of life, though, that she didn't feel like risking it in order to help her people.

This is when Esther's uncle, Mordecai, reminded her of her purpose.

> Do not imagine that you in the king's palace can escape any more than all the Jews. For if you remain silent at this time, relief and deliverance will arise for the Jews from another place and you and your father's house will perish. And who knows whether you have not attained royalty for such a time as this? (Esther 4:13-14).

In other words, "Esther, moving uptown had a purpose. It wasn't just about getting you out of the hood. Being pretty had a purpose. It wasn't just about you falling in love. God put you in a strategic position at a strategic time to fulfill a strategic purpose that is bigger than shopping and customizing your wardrobe."

Esther was to look at her life in terms of her destiny, not merely in terms of her money, status, image, house, and relationships. She was to view it in terms of her reason for living and her connection with God's kingdom and His agenda.

People who are serious about fulfilling the reason they were placed on earth will learn to view all of life through the grid of God's intentions. That worldview will then guide their decisions.

Lord, I want to view my life through Your eyes and Your intentions. Open my eyes so I can see what You are up to and know how I can join You in what You are doing. Open my eyes to see where You are working and how I fit in Your plan. I want You to use me, not someone else, for the purpose You have created me to fulfill.

Bad Decisions, Good Decisions

He said to me, "My grace is sufficient for you, for power is perfected
in weakness." Most gladly, therefore, I will rather boast about
my weaknesses, so that the power of Christ may dwell in me.

2 Corinthians 12:9

A young banker made an appointment to meet with the bank president, who was soon to retire. The younger man was in line to be the new president, and he was seeking advice as he prepared for his new responsibilities. He had one basic question: How had the older gentleman become so successful?

His predecessor looked at him and said two words: "Good decisions."

The young man, wanting more detail, pressed further and asked how one could come to make good decisions.

"Experience," his predecessor said.

The young banker continued his line of questioning. How could someone gain experience?

The older man replied, "Bad decisions."

Along the path to discovering your destiny, you are going to make some mistakes. You are going to suffer some setbacks. There will be times when you pause for a moment and say, "Why on earth did I do that?" Life is not perfect, and neither are you. There will be failures along with success. But how you respond to your bad decisions, mistakes, failures, and the like will determine in large part how well you achieve success.

If you let setbacks discourage you and allow doubt to seep into your thinking, you will postpone your future success. If you focus on the problems rather than the purpose to be learned from the problems, you may have to repeat those problems until you finally learn.

There is a learning curve to life, and it often includes experiences we would rather not have. But you can speed up that learning curve simply by viewing everything through the lens of God's purpose—and by trusting that God truly can work all things together for good if you will seek His heart in the midst of those experiences.

I want to learn from my failures, Lord, and not just dwell on them. Help me to see the wisdom to be gleaned from each one, and make me more Christlike through what I learn and apply.

The Divine Driver

After the earthquake a fire, but the LORD was not in the
fire; and after the fire a sound of a gentle blowing.

1 KINGS 19:12

When Jesus promises us, "He will guide you into all the truth" (John 16:13), that's a way of saying that the Holy Spirit will be the steering wheel of your life. There are two ways to get to a destination. One way is to look at the map and figure it out yourself as you drive. Another way is to have someone drive you who already knows where they are going.

If you have ever driven in an unfamiliar city or in a foreign land, you know that it is much easier to have someone drive you to your destination than for you to try to figure out the lane changes and sudden turns yourself. This is because they already know the way.

Why should our lives be any different? God already knows where He wants to take us. He knows the roads we need to travel on in order to reach our destiny. And He has given us His Holy Spirit who lives within us—our personal GPS to guide us on our journey.

The path to your destiny may have twists and turns that won't show up on a normal map, but the Holy Spirit even knows about those. As you seek to live your life on purpose, cultivate your relationship with the Spirit. Spend time in quiet every day listening for His voice. Discern how He speaks to you. It doesn't have to be long. You just need enough time to quiet your own mind and the thousands of thoughts racing through your head so you can recognize the still, small voice of God's Spirit. Try three minutes a day of silence for starters—not reciting items on a prayer list, but sitting in silence as you ask the Spirit to make His voice known to you. Over time you will begin to recognize His voice more clearly even in the midst of the busyness of life. And when you do, you will have tapped into the greatest Guide you could ever have on your journey to the fulfillment of your destiny.

....

Yours is a still small voice, yet it carries with it all that I need to know. I want to be able to discern Your voice more clearly. I *need* to be able to discern Your voice more clearly. Help me to do that.

A Doctor of Destiny

You are A CHOSEN RACE, A ROYAL PRIESTHOOD, A HOLY NATION,
A PEOPLE FOR God's OWN POSSESSION, so that you may
proclaim the excellencies of Him who has called you
out of darkness into His marvelous light.

1 PETER 2:9

Dr. Kenneth Cooper, the father of aerobics, was recognized at Harvard University with the Healthy Cup Award for "his dedication to understanding the scientific link between exercise and good health."*

Dr. Cooper also happens to be my doctor. I was sitting in his office one day, listening to him fuss at me like he normally does, when he began to tell me how his dream of creating a place that promotes preventative medicine through good health and fitness came into being.

"People think this is my job, Tony," he said. "They don't understand that this is my calling." Dr. Cooper went on to tell me he is not a medical doctor simply because he enjoys medicine. He said he chose to be a medical doctor because he was called by God to work in medicine. Medicine is his *ministry*. Roughly only 100,000 people jogged regularly when Dr. Cooper first published his bestselling book

---

* "'Father of Aerobics' Kenneth Cooper, MD, MPH to receive Healthy Cup Award from Harvard School of Public Health," *Harvard School of Public Health*, April 16, 2008, https://www.hsph.harvard.edu/news/press-releases/aerobics -kenneth-cooper-to-receive-harvard-healthy-cup-award.

Aerobics—introducing not only the word but also the concept into American culture.

Now, five decades later, that number exceeds 30 million. That is 30 million lives that are being strengthened and will have a better opportunity to fulfill their destinies. God is using Dr. Cooper's calling in connection with countless other people's destinies as well. His piece is part of a larger puzzle. And while Dr. Cooper's puzzle piece may seem significant due to his widespread influence, every person has a purpose to fulfill that is linked to God's greater goal.

That includes you, and the sooner you get to fulfilling that purpose, the sooner everyone else will benefit from your contribution to life. What is holding you back? It's time to move forward at full speed because God created you to do something that will bring you satisfaction and will empower others for good.

....

Whatever is holding me back from fully pursuing my purpose, Lord, I ask that You will help me to remove it or remove it for me. I want to do what You have put me on earth to do. I know that will bring me my greatest satisfaction and will bring good to others.

The Fifth Columnists

God, being rich in mercy, because of His great love with
which He loved us...raised us up with Him, and seated
us with Him in the heavenly places in Christ Jesus.

EPHESIANS 2:4,6

Have you ever heard of the term "fifth columnist"? No, it's not a writer for a newspaper. It's a term used in the military that goes back to the early twentieth century when the Spanish army general Emilio Mola Vidal termed a tactic that had been used for centuries.

As armies approached their target, the soldiers marched in four columns. The city being attacked could easily see the four columns coming. But what they didn't know about were the fifth columnists.

The fifth columnists had moved into the city sometime beforehand as covert operatives. They had become doctors and lawyers, politicians and businesspeople, infiltrating the land that would be attacked a year later.

In other words, they were saboteurs. They made preparations for the invasion. By the time the four columns marched, the fifth columnists would have already caused havoc on the inside. The four columns could do what they needed to do because of the subversives working internally.

God expects every Christian who is functioning in a business, a school, or our society at large to be a fifth columnist. As you live out your destiny, He expects you to be part of His army that works behind enemy lines to bring about His greater good. He wants you to represent the interests of heaven in the locality of earth where He has placed you.

Fifth columnists don't become part of the culture. They just function at the level they need to in order to help facilitate the bigger plan of their homeland. Always remember that your feet may be firmly planted on earth, but you are likewise seated in the heavenlies, and God wants you to be a part of causing His will to be done on earth as it is in heaven.

....

Dear God, I pray for Your insight as I go about my day so that I will know how to incorporate Your worldview into all that I do. Make me an instrument of good to everyone I come into contact with—those who do not yet know You as well as those who do.

A Vision of Time

He has made everything appropriate in its time.
He has also set eternity in their heart.

ECCLESIASTES 3:11

"Myopia" is the technical term for what is commonly known as near-sightedness. People who are nearsighted see only what's near or close to them. Their range of vision is limited. They need glasses to see things farther away.

This same medical terminology has been used in the broader context of life to describe people who are shortsighted and who don't see the big picture in life. Without a view of the big picture in life, it's easy to get distracted by what's right in front of you. It's easy to lose sight of your destiny because so much of your focus is on what's happening right now.

God wants you to look beyond today to all that He plans to accomplish in and through you during this process of living out your destiny.

The book of Ecclesiastes was written by a very busy man. Solomon controlled a large geographic area, led millions of people, entertained lavishly…simply keeping up with his hundreds of wives and concubines would have kept him very busy.

However, Solomon helps us to connect what we do with the way we spend our time. He puts our life in perspective. Ecclesiastes 3:1-8 emphasizes that there is a time for everything, and then verse 11 reveals the intended focal point of our purpose. He writes, "He has made everything appropriate in its time. He has also set eternity in their heart."

All of us have eternity in our hearts. We know there must be more to life than what we are experiencing right now. People who do not know God have eternal questions that they may spend a lifetime trying to answer: Who am I? Where am I going? Where did I come from?

Where do these questions come from? People ask them because God has placed eternity in their hearts.

If we lose sight of eternity because of a myopic focus on the present moment, we will lose out on the greater plan God has in store for us. When seeking and living out your destiny, always remember that it is inextricably tied to eternity.

....

Father, help me to keep eternity in mind, especially in the midst of worries I may have. If I waste my day worrying about things that are happening right now or could happen in the near future, I will miss out on the eternal purpose You have for me and that You are accomplishing in me. May I live every moment of every day in the light of eternity.

A Gift for You

To each one of us grace was given according to the measure of Christ's gift.

EPHESIANS 4:7

Many Christians fail to maximize their calling simply because they are not aware of their spiritual gifts. They may be stuck trying to utilize a talent rather than seeking God for the gifts He has given to them or discovering how God wants to transform their talents into gifts.

Other Christians fail to maximize their calling because they do not know that they even have a gift. But if you are a believer in Jesus Christ, you have a spiritual gift. In fact, you probably have several. God has equipped you with the necessary skills to fulfill the destiny for which You were made.

God will provide everything you need to do what He calls you to do. So if you are trying to do something you cannot do, either you are not in your calling, or you are not exercising the gift God has given to you and that He intends you to use. You can be sure God will prepare you to fulfill His purpose for you. Ephesians 4:7-8 says, "To each one of us grace was given according to the measure of Christ's gift. Therefore it says, 'WHEN HE ASCENDED ON HIGH, HE LED CAPTIVE A HOST OF CAPTIVES, AND HE GAVE GIFTS TO MEN.'"

In this passage, Paul affirms that "each one of us" has been given a gift. So there are no non-gifted Christians—either they are not actually Christians at all, or they don't yet know their spiritual endowment. If you are a Christian, you have a gift.

Not only do you have a gift, but that spiritual gift is uniquely tailored to your situation. Each one of us has a spiritual gift that is unique to our destiny and calling. I may have the same category of gift that you do, but it has not been given to accomplish the same purpose because each of us has a specific, personalized destiny. Your gift is yours and yours alone. If you do not know what it is, ask God to reveal it to you. If you do know, ask God to maximize its effectiveness so you can employ it to its fullest potential.

Lord, thank You for my spiritual gifts. Please continue to develop them through situations I face at work, in my home, at church...wherever. Open the doors that I need opened in order to use my gifts fully for Your glory and the fulfillment of my destiny.

Gifted to Serve

Let us consider how to stimulate one another to love and good deeds.

HEBREWS 10:24

Many Christians operate under the belief that the only people who have spiritual jobs to do are those who are called to preach, serve as missionaries, or sing or work in the church. But each saint has a gift that God has given him or her in order to build up His body. At the church where I've pastored for more than four decades, we have a requirement for those who want to become members. This requirement is that they agree to serve in some way in a ministry of the church. We do this not simply so we will have volunteers to sustain the more than 100 various ministries we have at our church, but more so, we do it so our members are held accountable to utilize their spiritual gifts.

I've seen many people in our church discover their spiritual gifts through this process of serving. Many have gone on to pursue professions in areas that they previously had not even realized they were gifted in. As a result, they are now not only strengthening the church, but they are also utilizing their gifts as salt and light in a needy world.

Your service is essential in the body of Christ because God wants His whole family to grow to maturity, and for that to happen, people who are gifted in different areas must contribute where they can. Your spiritual gift includes your whole person—your personality, passion, goals, skills, and more—but your spiritual gift was not given to you just for you.

God gave you your spiritual gift, or gifts, in order to be a blessing to others. The surefire way to keep God from blessing and maximizing His work in and through you is to stop your blessing *at* you. A blessing is always intended for the receiver to both enjoy and extend to others. Your gift is meant to bless the people around you.

....

God, make me an instrument that You can use for maximum impact. I offer my spiritual strengths, skills, and gifts for the advancement of Your kingdom. Sharpen my mind, soften my heart, and increase my passion to serve You at an even greater level than I do now.

Rebounds

I can do all things through Him who strengthens me.

PHILIPPIANS 4:13

In basketball, one of the most important skills a player can have is the ability to rebound.

Obviously, rebounds occur only after a missed shot—no miss, no need for a rebound. What causes players to miss field goals or free throws? One reason players miss shots is that their perspective can be off. They may have been looking at the goal, but they misjudged the distance or the angle or the timing. They were unable to sink the basket because there was not an accurate correlation between what they perceived and what they needed to do.

Another reason shots are missed in basketball games is that the opposing team is in a player's face. A defender's job is to wave their hands in the shooter's face and obstruct their view. They are supposed to provide a distraction.

Sometimes shots are missed because a player is fouled. Defenders commit fouls when they bump or shove the offensive players, preventing them from making the shot.

Coaches teach beginning players to follow their shots. In other words, after players shoot the ball, they should position themselves to go for a rebound if they miss. No player would walk off the court or throw in the towel because they have missed a shot. A good player will go back up for the ball and retrieve it and shoot again or pass to another player.

In the Bible, we find plenty of stories of people who missed shots. Many of God's servants missed their target and had to deal with the consequences of missing their shot. In fact, a study of the Word of God will reveal that God used many people who were on the rebound.

You may feel as if you've missed a shot or two along the way. We all do. The important thing to remember is this: Don't quit. Don't walk off the court. Don't throw in the towel. Go for the rebound, my friend, because God has a way of turning a missed shot into a miracle if you'll let Him.

....

Lord, You know I've blown it from time to time. You know better than I do when I've missed shots and what caused me to be off the mark. Please protect me from discouragement and despair. Direct my heart and my thoughts to You, for You are a God of rebounds.

Life in the Clouds

My flesh and my heart may fail,
But God is the strength of my heart and my portion forever.

PSALM 73:26

One day while flying his plane, a pilot noticed a small cloud up ahead. He decided to just fly through it. But once he got inside the cloud, he realized it wasn't as small as he had thought.

He decided to pull up and out of it, but after gaining quite a bit of altitude, he still wasn't in the clear. Next he decided to descend, confident the cloud didn't reach all the way to the ground. Again, no luck.

With all of his maneuvering, the pilot began to get a little disoriented. Sweat began pouring down his face because without any landmarks, he wasn't confident of his position. He started to feel upside down.

He checked his instruments, and they confirmed that the plane was still right side up. He felt as if the plane had tipped over, but the instruments said the opposite. The pilot made a decision to believe the instruments instead of his feelings. It took all of his energy to believe the instruments were functioning properly and telling him the truth.

Finally, he emerged from the cloud not far from the ground, because the cloud was low. When he came out, he was right side up. Had he believed what he felt, he would have been dead, but he acted on what the instruments said and not on his feelings.

Our emotions and feelings will often lead us into defeat, but the Word of God is an instrument that gives solid guidance and direction we can count on. Always adjust your feelings to your faith. Align your emotions with the truth of God's Word, and you will be on your way to fully living out the purpose God has for you.

Dear God, thank You for my emotions because they are an indicator of what I am thinking. When my thoughts are not aligned with Your Word, I am likely to worry, be afraid, or make rash decisions based on my feelings. I want to adjust my thoughts to Your Word, which will then adjust my feelings.

Moving Past Your Past

*I am well content with weaknesses, with insults, with
distresses, with persecutions, with difficulties, for Christ's
sake; for when I am weak, then I am strong.*

2 Corinthians 12:10

One difference between a successful person living out his or her destiny and a person aimlessly checking off each day is this: A successful person views his or her life experiences—the good as well as the bad—through the lens of purpose. They realize that God is able to use all of it to fulfill His calling on their lives.

An aimless person or bitter person cannot see the thread that connects life's experiences to his or her own destiny. These individuals' hearts may grow hard, their guilt may pile high, and they are often unable to move forward in life.

How you manage your past experiences will have everything to do with your future. The key is to learn from your past, not live in it. One of the easiest ways for Satan to keep you from moving forward is to get you to keep looking back. Are you the product of a dysfunctional family? God can use that for good. Did someone abuse or mistreat you? God can use that for good. Were you passed up for a promotion after years of dedicated service? God can use that for good. Has your marriage failed? Did your dreams come crashing down? Did you experience a betrayal from someone you trusted? Did you make some decisions as a teenager that are still affecting you two or three decades later?

Whatever is in your past—the good as well as the bad—God will use it for good if you will let Him. Resist the tendency to grow hard-hearted and bitter, and instead, choose a path that will help you move past your past. God wants to use the good and bad experiences of your life and to shape your destiny.

....

God, I don't want my heart to grow hard from the painful things I've experienced. I don't want to be bitter, cold, or jaded. Lord, help me to remember that You use it all for good when I let You…when I trust You. Help me to trust You more.

The Master Rebuilder

*If anyone is in Christ, he is a new creature; the old things
passed away; behold, new things have come.*

2 Corinthians 5:17

We can easily understand how God can use the good things in our
lives for His purposes. It is much more difficult to grasp how
a holy God can use our mistakes, failures, and sinful choices for His
good.

One of the greatest things about God's grace, though, is His ability
to turn a mess into a miracle. I'm not saying that God endorses mistakes or failures or that He accepts sin. He doesn't. But He can still
use those things to make us better for our destiny. Despite your failures, mistakes, and sins, God still has a blessing to give you and a destiny for you to fulfill.

Consider some ancient cities that have been destroyed and rebuilt.
Archaeologists tell us that parts of Jerusalem are built on 60 feet of rub-
ble. The hope of your Christian life is that Jesus Christ can take the
ruins of your life and make something new. The Bible is full of men
and women who failed and yet still discovered their destiny. God did
great things through many of these people, including Moses, Abraham, David, Sarah, Solomon, and Rahab.

You may have failed, but you are not a failure. That is not who you
are. In Christ, you are a new creation. God can use the mistakes of

your past to strengthen you for a brighter tomorrow. Seek God in your mess. Let Him know you are not proud of it, you wish you could undo it, but since it is there and it is done—you are asking Him to turn it around in order to use it for good.

God can use the bad for good. Let Him. Make yourself available to His grace and to His mercy. He has a plan for you.

I am a new creation in You, Lord. You make all things new. Thank You for new beginnings, new days and opportunities to begin again. I trust that You will give me grace where I need it and favor for my future because of the great love and sacrifice of my Savior, Jesus Christ.

How Not to Get a Promotion

Whatever you do, do your work heartily, as
for the Lord rather than for men.

COLOSSIANS 3:23

Imagine a person saying to their boss, "I know I've been doing a sloppy job, but I have a good reason. It's because you haven't given me a promotion. If you would promote me, I wouldn't do a sloppy job. So here's what I recommend—you give me that promotion, and then you'll see how I can really work!"

Not only would that person not receive a promotion, they would soon be job hunting. Why? Because that's not how it works. I've never heard or seen it work like that in the workplace, and I bet you never have either. Promotions typically come through faithfulness, tenacity, commitment, and results.

Yet far too often that is the way we bargain with God. We want Him to take us to the next level of His plan for us before we commit to or master the level we are currently on. Maybe we do this because we don't particularly care for His current assignment for us. It could be that it isn't very exciting, noteworthy, or fun. It might be mundane or even difficult work. But God has a reason for every season of your life—nothing is for naught.

Sometimes your assignment is intended to test you; other times it is meant to train you. Perhaps God is using your work to develop a deeper level of faithfulness and commitment within you. Whatever it is, God has a reason for you being right where you are now.

If you are not enjoying the stage of life God has you in right now, don't complain. Rather, work harder. Do all that you do to the very best of your abilities and with a grateful heart while asking Him to take you to the next level. God is watching your external actions just as much as He is watching your internal mindset. Let Him hear your thankfulness for what you have to be grateful for even if you are wanting Him to move you further in your destiny. Gratitude, rather than complaining, is God's recipe for success. Use it, practice it, make it a daily—even hourly—habit, and then keep your eyes peeled for where God is taking you.

Lord, I want my focus to be on You and not on my job, my supervisors, or any other aspect of my current situation. I want to please You in this season You have me in, so I thank You for the myriad of good things You have given to me, including the ability to read Your Word, understand what You are saying to me, and seek You in all I do.

On Watching a Parade

Without faith it is impossible to please Him, for he who comes to God must believe that He is and that He is a rewarder of those who seek Him.

HEBREWS 11:6

As you travel down the road to your destiny, always keep in mind that God is very different from us. That seems obvious, but it's easy to forget if you begin to focus on your circumstances rather than on Him.

One of the major differences between God and us is that we have different viewpoints. Take a parade, for example. We watch a parade progressively. We watch one band come down the path after another. We watch the parade go by one entry at a time.

Yet God sees the whole parade at the same time. God is not bound in time the way we are. He doesn't have to wait for each float to turn the corner. From the starting point to the finish, He sees the whole parade. He sees the whole package. That's why "without faith it is impossible to please God." You've got to believe He sees what you can't. You've got to believe His perspective includes the entire event even though you can't see around the corner.

It's easy to be worried, sad, or disappointed when things don't go your way. But when that happens, remember that this particular segment of time is not the whole story. It's just a part of the parade; it's not the whole parade. God doesn't struggle with disappointment, fear, and worry, because He knows the end from the beginning. He knows what's next and how each piece connects.

Has something ever happened to you that you wished had never happened…only to discover some months or years later that it was a positive thing after all? Had it not happened, you wouldn't have learned an important lesson, or you wouldn't have gotten to the next stage of your journey or started an important relationship. Whatever it was, hindsight changed your perspective—you now valued what once disappointed you.

In pursuing and living out your destiny, always give God the benefit of the doubt because His perspective is like no other—He knows all, and it all makes sense to Him. Trust Him, even when you can't see what's up ahead. After all, God does some of His best work in the dark.

Lord, give me the kind of faith that pleases You. Grant me Your grace and favor so that I may grow in this area and truly trust You in all that I do and in all that happens to me.

Let Go

He was oppressed and He was afflicted,
Yet He did not open His mouth;
Like a lamb that is led to slaughter,
And like a sheep that is silent before its shearers,
So He did not open His mouth.

ISAIAH 53:7

The story is told about a man who was collecting eggs from a nest on the side of a very steep cliff. As he carefully approached the nest, he slipped and started to slide over the edge of the cliff. At the last second, he was able to grab a branch and stop his plunge to the valley below.

Dangled over the precipice, hundreds of feet in the air, he screamed, "Help me! Somebody help me!"

A voice came out of the sky, "Do you believe I can help you?"

The man responded, "Yes, I believe. Please help me!"

The voice came out of the sky again. "Do you believe I have the power to help you?"

"Yes, I believe! I believe! Please help me!"

"Do you believe I love you enough to help you?"

"Yes, I know You love me. Please, oh please, HELP ME!"

"Because you believe, I will help you. Now let go."

After a brief silence, the man said, "Is there anybody else up there?"

God doesn't always make sense, does He? Throughout Scripture and church history, He has asked people to do things that don't make sense—such as let go of whatever they were holding on to for dear life. He asked Abraham to let go of Isaac and the promise of a blessed generation. He asked Ruth to let go of familiarity and her homeland in exchange for the unknown. He asked Joseph to let go of judgment and suspicion when Mary became pregnant.

God may be asking you to let go of something you hold dear—a person, a job, or perhaps a mindset—because He knows in letting go, you will have the opportunity to demonstrate great faith. And great faith always produces a great return.

Is God prompting you to trust Him with something today? Letting go may be the very thing that will take you to the next step toward your destiny.

....

Jesus, thank You for Your example of letting go and trusting Your Father. In the face of great pain and separation, You did not complain. At the cross, You let go of Your own wants and desires and submitted Yourself to God. May I have the grace to let go of whatever I am clinging to—without complaining and with a heart full of love for You.

Faith in a Big God

The eternal God is a dwelling place,
And underneath are the everlasting arms.

Deuteronomy 33:27

Two business partners had to travel to a small town for a very important meeting that held great potential for their company—and for their careers. The problem was that the small town was located some distance from a major airport. The only flights in and out of this town were on small twin-engine prop planes.

A few days before the meeting, one of the businessmen told the other, "I've decided not to go."

"What! Why not?" asked the partner.

"I am not getting on one of those tiny planes." Apparently, the size of this man's faith was tied to the size of the plane. When the plane got smaller, his faith got smaller.

So the business partner traveled to the meeting alone, and it ended up being a game-changer. He was offered a new partnership with the people he had gone to meet with. He was offered a greater salary and a larger stake in the new company than what he had before. He was given greater influence and a greater return on his investment of both time and money. The offer would have gone to both of them had the business partner shown enough faith to fly in the small plane. But because he didn't, the offer only went to the one. And the business partner who decided to stay home out of fear lost that which was most dear to him.

God is a big God, and He is worthy of your faith. But when your view of God is small, you won't have the courage to go wherever He wants you to go. You will limit yourself through fear. And you will miss out on all He has stored up for you. If your faith is small, your return is small. Do you want a large destiny? Then have large faith.

Dear God, increase my faith in ways I have never imagined. I want to experience You fully and know You, and I know my experience will broaden along with my faith. Show me how to trust in You more and more each day.

Every Day a Special Day

If you abide in Me, and My words abide in you,
ask whatever you wish, and it will be done for you.

JOHN 15:7

Some husbands give their wives an anniversary present every year. The husband comes home from work, takes his wife out to dinner, gives her a great gift, and makes a big deal about that special day—but only once a year. The wife doesn't receive much love, affection, and appreciation from him for the rest of the year.

The husband doesn't regularly take her out for dinner. There are no dates. There is no romance. But she knows that next year on their anniversary, there is going to be another great present, a nice date, and some kind words.

What do you think? Do you think those wives are satisfied with that relationship? Or do you think they would gladly trade a big anniversary celebration for 365 days of love and tenderness and open communication?

My decades of marital counseling would lead me to conclude that those wives are not satisfied with a once-a-year display of affection. They would rather have an ongoing romantic relationship instead of just one big event a year.

Yet that's what so many of us do with God. We do one big thing for Him and then say, "There You go, God. See, I love You." And then we return to our normal life, looking out for our own personal needs and desires before His. Talking with our friends more than communicating with Him. Eating what we enjoy rather than spending time in fasting and prayer before our Creator and Sustainer.

Yet God is a God of relationship. He is a God of communion, and He longs to be close to you. He appreciates the occasional biggies you do for Him, but much more, He desires your consistent obedience and ever-deepening relationship. He wants to know you truly love and value Him—not just for what He can do for you, but for who He is.

God longs for you to fully live out the plan and destiny He has created for you. But that can happen only in the context of a relationship with Him. In Scripture, that's called "abiding," and it is one of the most strategic and satisfying things you could ever do.

My desire is to be near You, Lord, as You desire to be near me. But I often get distracted with the circumstances of life that surround me. Remind me when I am away from You mentally or spiritually so that I can return to a place of nearness to You.

Jumping into Your Destiny

Immediately Jesus stretched out His hand and took hold of him,
and said to him, "You of little faith, why did you doubt?"

MATTHEW 14:31

I love the Olympics. I love to watch athletes at their peak physical fitness competing with each other. It is fun to see people fully maximizing their talent, training, and strength.

I enjoy watching the high jumpers in the track and field portion of the Olympics. In 1993, at a different meet, Javier Sotomayor of Cuba cleared the bar at an amazing 8 feet—a record that has stood for 25 years.

I also enjoy watching the pole-vaulters. The Olympic men's record stands at nearly 20 feet. When pole-vaulters begin a jump, they take a step back, look down the runway, and sprint toward the bar, carrying an enormous pole. When they reach the end of the track, they stick the pole in a special box set in the ground. As they swing their legs off the ground, the pole acts like a spring and propels them high into the air. Because they rely on the pole, they go higher than they possibly could on their own.

What God has created you to fulfill—your destiny—is beyond you. Your own skill, strength, and smarts are not enough for you to reach your destiny on your own. In fact, if your destiny is not bigger than you, it's not actually your destiny. It's simply you trying to make it on your own. God works where there is faith, and faith believes in what is beyond your own ability to understand or accomplish.

When reaching for your destiny, you need something like a pole-vaulter's pole—something that will propel you higher than you could go on your own. That pole is faith. It is faith in God's Word, faith in His character, and faith that He will do what He has said He will do. Use the pole of faith to get where you need to go. When you do, you will learn how to soar.

....

God, I trust that faith will take me further than I could ever go on my own. Faith is the substance of things hoped for, the evidence of things not seen. Increase my faith, God, where it is lacking. I want to please You with my faith.

The Junkyard Master

These things I have spoken to you, so that in Me you may have peace. In the world you have tribulation, but take courage; I have overcome the world.

JOHN 16:33

I know a man named Billy who lives in a nearby town. Billy is what you might call a junkyard specialist. Billy spends his time going to junkyards around the area and looking at the things other people have thrown away. He scours the junkyards to find value in that which has been deemed worthless.

Billy then loads his treasures into his truck and hauls them back to his garage. In his garage, he turns what was once considered junk into contemporary pieces of art. He then sells them to interested buyers for up to $5,000.

Billy can do this because he sees more than what everyone else sees. When Billy looks at junk, he sees a masterpiece in the making.

When God sees you, mistakes and all, He also sees a masterpiece. You may feel worthless, used up, or discarded. But when you met Jesus Christ, you met the One who can transform you from what you think you are into what you truly are—a valuable masterpiece with a purpose.

Billy's artwork does more than fill empty spaces with interesting ornaments. Billy's pieces are conversation starters. When people look at one of Billy's works, they ask the owner to tell them the story behind it. The owner then explains how Billy went about crafting the marvel. In other words, Billy's art brings him glory.

Similarly, you are to be a conversation starter about your Creator. You are here to bring God glory. You have a story to tell. You have a life to share. Your experiences and the situations you face not only shape you into who you are but also provide a testimony to encourage others along their way as well.

Never be shy about telling others how God has brought you to where you are today. Your story matters, and it can make a difference in the lives of those around you.

....

Dear God, thank You for taking the mess and mistakes of my past and weaving them all together to create the masterpiece You have called me to be. I embrace Your plan for my life and trust You will bring it about in complete fruition of Your intention.

An Intentional Life

*Worthy are You, our Lord and our God, to receive glory
and honor and power; for You created all things, and
because of Your will they existed and were created.*

REVELATION 4:11

When God creates a life, He has an intention for that life. When He created you, He did so with intention. God doesn't make mistakes. He is sovereign over everything, including the creation of life. This means that nothing comes to you that does not pass through God's fingers first—including your very existence. When God created you, He sovereignly chose where you would be born, who you would be, and what His purpose for your life would be.

That does not mean that everyone always achieves God's destiny for their lives. Many do not seek Him, trust Him, or pursue His purpose in their lives. But God created everyone with a destiny that would blow their minds if they only knew what God wanted them to do.

Unfortunately, people often get hung up on things that appear to make no sense. They get stuck trying to figure out why bad things happen to good people. They fall into a rut of doubt or self-pity because they have lost sight of their destiny. Without a strong faith in God's sovereignty, we can easily get sidelined and distracted from what God has put us here to do.

Keep in mind that believing in God's sovereignty does not mean you believe He causes everything in your life. Rather, it means that God either causes *or allows* everything in your life. And if He allows it, He can use it. Trusting in His sovereignty means trusting that He can cause everything to work for your good—even the confusing and hurtful things—if you choose to love Him and respond to Him in the calling of your destiny.

You are not a mistake. You were made on purpose for a purpose. Embrace that truth and start living in light of it.

Lord, You created all things, and they exist for You. This includes me. You have made me with a purpose in mind, and I want to fulfill it. I want to live my purpose each and every day. Thank You for giving me a unique purpose and for enabling me to fulfill it.

Power in Your Personality

*God...set me apart even from my mother's womb
and called me through His grace.*

GALATIANS 1:15

Your personality is the part of you that makes you the person you are. Just as no two people have the same thumbprints, no two people have exactly the same personality. God gave you the personality you have because it fits perfectly with the destiny He has planned for you. If you have to become somebody else in order to fulfill a certain purpose, then God wants somebody else to do it. That's not your purpose or your destiny. God made your personality to fit your destiny. Your destiny has been designed to fit who you are.

Take a look at several of the personalities in the Bible. Peter was the impetuous, self-proclaimed leader and spokesperson. He was always putting his foot in his mouth and speaking whatever came to his mind. God used Peter's personality to empower him to fulfill his destiny—to announce the beginning of the church. Paul, on the other hand, was a studious thinker. God used him to write much of the theology in the New Testament. John was the loving and intimate personality who leaned his head on Jesus and had a close relationship with Him. God used John to write about the power of abiding in Christ and the importance of loving relationships (1 John 3–4).

Throughout Scripture, God used people's personalities to help them fulfill their destinies. God's calling is consistent with how He made you. You don't need to change your personality to pursue your destiny. In fact, a healthy awareness of who you are and how God made you will give you insight into how He wants to use you.

Lord, thank You for my personality. Thank You for the unique traits that make me who I am. Use my personality for Your glory as You empower me to fulfill the destiny You have created for me.

Letting Go

As for you, you meant evil against me, but God meant it for good in order to bring about this present result, to preserve many people alive.

GENESIS 50:20

The patriarch Joseph spoke the words above after reuniting with his brothers, who had rejected him and sold him into slavery. Amazingly, Joseph didn't allow bitter events or bitter people to keep him from fulfilling his destiny. Though he was mistreated again and again, he remained confident God used those painful experiences for his good—and for the good of those around him.

I know it hurts when people turn against you. But like Joseph, you can let go of bitterness. God allowed those negative people and those negative circumstances to make you who you are today. Just as God had a plan for Joseph, He has a plan to use all of the ugly stuff in your life for good. Somewhere down the line, He will work through you to help someone else who has been hurt, abandoned, lied about, or broken...someone who is looking for hope.

View your pain theologically, not socially. Don't just say, "That's not fair." Rather, say, "God, even though that's not fair, I believe You are going to use it so I can fulfill my destiny. I trust You to use the bitter things in my life and use them for Your glory."

You may very well be right—it probably wasn't fair. That terrible thing that happened to you that you had no control over—it's not fair.

But God is a master at turning unfair things into miracles when we let Him. Don't block His work in your life by harboring bitterness, anger, and hate. Instead, tell Him that what happened wasn't fair—and then tell Him you are going to let it go anyway. Then sit back and watch how He uses it for good. God is a just God. Let Him have it. He will bring about justice if you step out of the way and let Him. Trust Him with the deepest, most authentic faith you have.

God can make the bitter things in your life better. He can make the good things great. He can cover the bad with His grace. The good, the bad, and the bitter can all come together to lead you to your destiny.

Lord, You know I don't like painful things in my life. I don't like the ways I have been hurt. But I know You can use them for good if I will let go of bitterness and resentment and trust You instead.

Meaning in the Mundane

Do not fear; you are more valuable than many sparrows.

MATTHEW 10:31

As you are carrying out the normal routines in your life, God is setting up situations and intersections for you to walk into. He is preparing you for the destiny and future He has for you, and He is also preparing others for you. He is creating perfect scenarios for situations and people to connect at just the right time, leading you to fulfill your destiny.

You may think you are in a dead-end career right now. Or perhaps you see no end to changing diapers, washing clothes, and chauffeuring your children around to their different events. Perhaps you had a dream in your heart—a passion—for quite some time, and yet you see no real connection between that dream and your current daily activities.

If you feel that way, remember that God will often use intersections in life to get you to where you need to go.

An intersection is a place where things converge. When you reach an intersection while driving, cars coming from one direction converge with cars coming from another direction. They intersect.

One way to discover your destiny is to watch the pieces of your life intersect in a divinely ordained way. Keep your eyes open for the intersections of life. Perhaps it's someone you meet, a skill set you pick up, or a place you go. In the process of getting you where you need to go, God will frequently bring you to intersections where you find pieces and parts you'll need along the way. Even if the intersection doesn't make sense at the time, you can be confident that God has a plan in store.

That's why the mundane circumstances of your life—your daily routines—aren't actually mundane at all. Seemingly insignificant intersections of life can carry the greatest value in the long run.

God is leading you from where you are to where He wants you to be—where the divine intersection of your gifts, skills, passion, experience, and purpose merge. Even now He is preparing you for that place…and preparing that place for you.

....

Holy Father, life has so many parts and pieces to it—so many conversations, events, thoughts, and circumstances. Help me to make sense of what I can. And help me to trust You with the rest, knowing that You are sovereign over all.

Informative Intersections

Elisha prayed and said, "O LORD, I pray, open his eyes that he may see."
And the LORD opened the servant's eyes and he saw; and behold,
the mountain was full of horses and chariots of fire all around Elisha.

2 KINGS 6:17

When you are seeking God, you don't have to worry about finding your destiny. Your destiny will find you. You will discover it in the divine intersections God has planned for you.

Time after time the Bible gives us illustrations of divine intersections.

- The infant Moses's intersection with Pharaoh's daughter on the Nile positioned him to eventually set God's people free.

- Beautiful Abigail offered David's army some food just in time to stop a rampage on her home. Abigail's foolish husband later died, and she became the king's wife.

- Ruth gleaning in Boaz's field set her up to become a matriarch in the line of Jesus Christ.

- When Queen Esther's husband couldn't sleep and asked for something to read, he was brought the book of history, and he heard the account of Mordecai saving him. This eventually led to the Israelites' empowerment to defend themselves against their enemies and escape annihilation.

You never know how God is going to bring things together at just the right time. Intersections are happening all around you, but you need to be on the lookout in order to notice them. When things don't make sense, rather than complaining or giving up, ask yourself, "Why has God led me here? What might He be adding to my life? How might this help me fulfill my destiny?" Questions like these will help you receive the most benefit from the divine intersections in your life.

Lord, open my eyes so that I may truly see what is going on all around me. Help me to see the spiritual realm and not just the physical. Please increase my spiritual insight and wisdom.

The Report from Above

As the heavens are higher than the earth,
So are My ways higher than your ways
And My thoughts than your thoughts.

ISAIAH 55:9

Urban commuters often check traffic reports before they head out onto the roads to go to work. The reports let them know which freeways are clogged up, which routes are best to take, and how much time they need to reach their destination.

Many traffic reports are given from helicopters. A reporter looks down at the whole situation and gives real-time direction to drivers so they know how to proceed.

Drivers could say, "I'm not going to listen to the traffic report. I'm going to take my chances." The problem is, if they get stuck in traffic, they won't be able to see what's going on. All they will see is a long line of cars.

Now, which is better? Does it make more sense to try making the traffic decision on your own and risk getting stuck, or does it make more sense to follow the instructions from a traffic reporter in a helicopter? Of course, listening to the reporter makes more sense because he or she is high overhead and can see the big picture.

The same is true for living out your destiny. From God's vantage point, He sees it all—the beginning, the middle, and the end. He knows where all the roads go, which ones will lead to setbacks, and which ones can get you to your destination the fastest. In fact, God knows some shortcuts or detours that will get you to your destiny quicker than you even imagined.

Do you want to try figuring out all of this on your own? Or will you seek His heart and His hand by spending time reading His Word and communing with His Holy Spirit? The latter will get you to the full manifestation of your destiny faster than anything else ever could.

Gracious and all-knowing God, Your ways are higher than my ways—they go beyond my understanding. I pray that I will follow You rather than my own inclinations in all I do.

Your Control Tower

All Scripture is inspired by God and profitable for teaching,
for reproof, for correction, for training in righteousness.

2 TIMOTHY 3:16

Before airplanes take off from a large airport, the pilots need to be in communication with air traffic controllers who are seated high above in a control tower. The air traffic controllers can see what the pilots cannot. The pilots have a limited vantage point. They can't see underneath or above them. The pilots, even with all of their instruments, can't see the air traffic around the airport. The tower can provide the pilots information they wouldn't have because of their limited vantage point.

The Word of God is your control tower. Where you have only a limited vantage point, God's Word can communicate to you what is going on in the spiritual realm that you can't see. Discovering and living out your destiny on a daily basis involves ongoing time in God's Word. God uses His Word to give wisdom and guidance, especially when it takes root and grows in your spirit.

Of course, God's Word will never tell you whether you should take a certain job, marry a certain person, or move to a certain town. But God uses His Word to speak to you about these things in various ways. This is called God's *rhema* word. The Holy Spirit applies the *logos* (the written Word of God) to specific areas of your life.

God's Word is a treasure trove of guidance and grace. Never view it simply as a historical book filled with God's truth. View it as a tool God has given to you to direct your steps as you walk down this path toward your destiny.

....

Father, thank You for Your Word—both Your written Word and Your *rhema* word that the Holy Spirit communicates to my spirit to inform me, guide me, and direct me. Give me a hunger to know You and to know Your Word in a deeper way.

Redeeming the Time

Be careful how you walk, not as unwise men but as wise,
making the most of your time, because the days are evil.

<small>Ephesians 5:15-16</small>

The book of Ecclesiastes tells us that "there is an appointed time for everything. And there is a time for every event under heaven" (Ecclesiastes 3:1). It also says that God "has made everything appropriate in its time" (verse 11).

God has a clock. Yet God Himself is not obligated to follow the clock because God is eternal. God moves freely in and out of the clock.

However, you and I are obligated to follow the clock because we are still bound by time. That's why Paul tells us in his letter to the church at Ephesus, "Therefore be careful how you walk, not as unwise men but as wise, *making the most of your time*, because the days are evil. So then do not be foolish, but understand what the will of the Lord is" (Ephesians 5:15-17).

The King James Version calls this "redeeming the time." We are to make the most of the time we have, not wasting it or squandering it by not understanding God's purpose for our time.

Time has been given to you for one reason—so you can fulfill your destiny. If you are still alive and you still have time, then that time has been given to you so you can achieve the destiny God has ordained for you.

Time is consistent with destiny and purpose.

When you have to get up and go to work in the morning, you will set your clock to 6:00 a.m. or whatever time you choose that will get you to your destination on schedule. This is because time is tied to purpose. Therefore, if you do not live on purpose, you will not use your time wisely. You will get up anytime you feel like it, go to bed anytime, and let the days slip by without redeeming the time. And before you know it, you are 50, 60, or 70 years old, and you wonder, "Where did all the time go?"

Your time and the way you use it are intimately linked with purpose and destiny. Knowing and living your purpose gives you God's perspective on the use of your time.

Dear Lord, help me to make the most of the time You have given me. Show me how my choices result in me wasting the time You have given me or using it in line with the purpose for which You have created me.

A Contribution or a Sacrifice?

If anyone wishes to come after Me, he must deny himself, and take up his cross daily and follow Me. For whoever wishes to save his life will lose it, but whoever loses his life for My sake, he is the one who will save it.

LUKE 9:23-24

One day, a chicken and a pig were walking down the street when they arrived at a grocery store. A sign in the window of the store read, Needed: Bacon and Eggs. The chicken and the pig looked at each other.

The chicken said, "I'll give him the eggs if you give him the bacon."

"You have to be crazy," said the pig. "Have you lost your mind?"

"What's the problem?" asked the chicken.

The pig replied, "The problem is that for you it is a contribution. But for me, it's my life!"

A lot of people today want to give God a contribution. They will give an egg here or there—or maybe a dozen from time to time. But they don't want to climb up on the altar and die to their own wants, desires, dreams, and will so they can be maximized for God's purpose as living sacrifices. But God doesn't want your eggs. He wants your pork chops, ham hocks, and pigs' feet. He wants the whole deal.

Living a life of destiny means just that—living a whole life of destiny. It does not mean living a day or an hour of it. Too many people today want to be part-time Christians but expect God to give them a full-time blessing. That mentality wouldn't go very far on your job, and it certainly doesn't go far with God either.

Are you giving God a contribution of your time, talents, and treasures, or are you giving Him your all? You will be amazed when you surrender your all to Him—He will flood you with satisfaction and purpose. True happiness is found in being who you were created to be.

Father, I surrender my life to You. Use me at the fullest capacity possible. I give You my heart, my goals, and my dreams, and I ask that You will bring about the complete expression of the destiny You have created me to fulfill.

A Transformed Mind

*Do not be conformed to this world, but be transformed by the
renewing of your mind, so that you may prove what the will
of God is, that which is good and acceptable and perfect.*

ROMANS 12:2

If you are to reach your destiny, the world cannot own you. Rather,
you must commit *all of you* to *all of God*. You must belong to Him.
When you belong to God, you will be "transformed by the renewing
of your mind." The Greek word used for "transformed" is in the passive tense. This means that the transformation is not something you
do for yourself; God does it for you.

For example, if I were to tell you I drove to the store, I would be
using an active construction to describe something I did. However, if I
told you I was driven to the store, I would be using a passive construction to explain that someone else did something for me.

In other words, when you commit your life to God and give Him
all of you, not allowing the world to have anything of you, you have
positioned yourself so the Holy Spirit can go to work in your mind.
He will do the work if you will position yourself rightly underneath
God as a living and holy sacrifice.

Rather than being double-minded (James 1:5-8), or rather than
living in spiritual schizophrenia, you will have a clear mind because
of the Spirit's work within you. As the Spirit begins to work in your

mind, transforming it, He will reveal the will of God to you. "As he thinks within himself, so he is" (Proverbs 23:7). The Holy Spirit will reveal to you the steps you are to take, the thoughts you are to think, and the path you are to follow in order to completely live out and experience the abundance and joy that comes from fulfilling your destiny.

....

God in heaven, transform my mind with the work of the Holy Spirit. I commit my thoughts to You so that You can replace my wrong thinking with Your truth. You know the path I am to take, so I trust You to give me thoughts that are in line with what You are doing.

A Valley of Development

Now then go, and I, even I, will be with your
mouth, and teach you what you are to say.

Exodus 4:12

The book of Exodus contains one of the greatest biblical stories related to destiny.

Most of us are familiar with Moses. We know how he floated in a basket along the Nile until Pharaoh's daughter found him. We know about the ten plagues and the parting of the Red Sea. We know that he led the Israelites out of bondage and into freedom.

However, we can easily miss the significance of what happened during a period of Moses's life that the Bible says very little about. Not much is written concerning the time between Moses's fortieth year (when he fled from Egypt) until his eightieth year (when he met God at the burning bush). Even though there isn't much written about those four decades, they are critical. During those years, Moses experienced the development he needed to fulfill his destiny.

The road to your destiny passes through a valley of development. This is where God prepares you for your destiny and prepares everything and everyone else related to your destiny for you.

Most of us don't like to think about going through a time of development. It doesn't usually make for the greatest stories in the Bible either. When we consider Moses, we recall things like the Red Sea or the burning bush. But Moses's destiny didn't begin there. It began long before those events. It started in a time of preparation. It began during many long and drawn-out days when Moses took care of things that did not seem all too spectacular. He shepherded sheep each day and ate his meals by a fire each night. His preparation began in trials, challenges, and boredom.

And just as God had a plan for Moses, He has a plan to prepare you and lead you to your destiny. He also has a plan to prepare you as well. A developmental process must occur so that when you arrive at your bush, you are ready for your calling and, just as importantly, your calling and all that it entails are ready for you.

Lord, I ask that You will help me to cherish each moment, even those moments when nothing spectacular seems to be happening. Help me to see meaning where I cannot right now, knowing that You are always working in my situation and developing me for what's ahead.

A Voice in the Silence

My sheep hear My voice, and I know them, and they follow Me.

JOHN 10:27

One day, a Native American from a rural village decided to visit a friend in New York City. As they walked together down the bustling sidewalk, the Native American Indian suddenly held up his hand. They paused, and he asked his friend, "Do you hear that?"

"Hear what?" his friend asked over the sounds of cars and buses, a bit bewildered.

"It's a cricket," the Native American said.

"A cricket?" his friend replied. "I don't hear a cricket. In fact, how is it even possible to hear a cricket over the roar of the traffic?"

The Native American walked over to the street corner, where a small cricket was sitting. He leaned over and scooped it up, much to the amazement of his friend.

The Native American smiled and led his friend to a group of people standing nearby. He reached in his pocket, grabbed some change, and dropped it on the ground. As the coins hit the ground, several heads turned.

The Native American Indian turned toward his friend with a smile and said, "You hear what you want to hear."

When we don't hear God, the problem is not that He isn't talking, but that we're not attuned to the sound of His voice. God could stand before many of us and shout, and yet we wouldn't hear Him simply because we wouldn't recognize His voice.

If you are pursuing your destiny, one basic necessity you must incorporate into your lifestyle is a regular time of silence. You don't need to become a monk and move into a monastery, but you do need to find times when you can quiet the extra noise in your life so you can hear God's voice. You also need to learn how to quiet the noise within you—your constant stream of thoughts—so you can hear God.

Prayer is a great way to practice this by spending time actively listening to the Lord. Even if you don't hear anything at all, that time is valuable because you are cultivating the virtue of listening. God longs to speak to you, so make sure you are positioned to hear Him when He does.

Lord, help me to listen. I want to listen to You, but it's easy to be distracted by the noise of this world and the thoughts that race through my own head. I commit to spending moments of quiet before You, Lord. Please honor my commitment by teaching me how to best hear You when You speak to me.

In the Driver's Seat

Eli said to Samuel, "Go lie down, and it shall be if He calls you, that you shall say, 'Speak, LORD, for Your servant is listening.'" So Samuel went and lay down in his place.

1 SAMUEL 3:9

When my children were small, we sometimes went to the empty church parking lot on Saturday nights, and I let them "drive" the car. They took turns sitting on my lap and steering the wheel. But they didn't know that while they were driving, I was actually running the show. My foot was on the brake or the accelerator, and no matter where they had their hands on the wheel, I held the bottom of it with two fingers to control how far they could turn it. They weren't going to go too fast. Nor were they going to go anywhere they shouldn't.

In other words, they positioned themselves to go somewhere, but I controlled where they went. As a result, they had a much better experience than they would have if they had driven on their own.

As you continue along your path of destiny, be sure to always position yourself as close to God as possible. When you place yourself near Him, in His presence, you are more likely to have a tremendous ride in this life. You won't discover your destiny when you function independently of God.

When you get close to Him, you will hear Him call you by name, just as He called Samuel. Samuel was in the house of the Lord, the temple, when he heard God call, "Samuel!" (1 Samuel 3:6).

God has a calling, a destiny, with your name on it. I can't tell you what it is because I don't know. But I do know that your destiny will always incorporate your passion, vision, gifts, experience, and opportunities. It will also light a fire in you when you hear it, see it, or do it.

You will know your destiny when you hear the Spirit speak it with your name on it. And when you do, respond with all you have within you.

Speak, Lord, for Your servant is listening. Whisper in my ear Your plans and Your path for me. Take control of the wheel of my life so that I may go where You want me to go.

The Truth

You will know the truth, and the truth will make you free.

JOHN 8:32

People often want objective standards. Imagine laying on an operating table in your last few moments of consciousness and hearing your surgeon say, "Hmm...I think this is where I need to cut. Other doctors have ideas of where to cut, but this is what I think. Let's just check it out and see what happens." Would you trust that doctor?

Or suppose your pharmacist said, "Let's see...I think this is the medicine you should take. The pharmacist down the street disagrees, but this is what I think. Why don't you just give it a try?"

Or picture yourself boarding a plane and hearing the pilot say, "Um...I think this is the button I'm supposed to push. My engineer thinks I ought to push this button on the left, and my copilot thinks I should push a button over here on the right. The flight attendant thinks I should push a different one. Well...let's try this button and see if it gets us off the ground."

That wouldn't be good enough, would it? At the doctor's office, you want truth. At the pharmacist's, you want truth. In the airplane, you want truth. You don't want a pilot saying, "I think..." or a doctor saying, "I have a pretty good idea..." or a pharmacist saying, "I have a hunch." You want these people to know for sure.

Everyone wants their doctor or pharmacist or pilot to tell them the truth, yet many people seem unconcerned about knowing God's truth. His truth—the absolute standard of reality found in His Word—is all you need in order to discover and fully live out your destiny. The truth of God is the foundation of your life. Read His Word. Memorize it. Meditate on it. Know it. Apply it. Then watch it bear fruit as you live out the purpose He has for you.

Lord, thank You for being a God of truth and for never changing like a shifting shadow. Thank You for being fully and completely trustworthy. Your Word is truth, and it is a lamp for my feet. I praise You for making this available to me and for giving me such an enormous treasure—Your Word.

Deep Cleansing

Therefore there is now no condemnation for those who are in Christ Jesus.

ROMANS 8:1

Just before I go to the dentist, I make sure to do an especially good job of brushing my teeth. I spend extra time scrubbing and flossing to make a good impression with the dentist.

The problem is, my dentist is rarely impressed by my efforts that day. He's not satisfied with one good brushing or one careful flossing. He looks deeper. He takes X-rays of my teeth and then uses special tools to clean between them. Consequently, he finds stuff I never even knew was there.

I thought I had taken care of everything on my own, but the dentist finds things I missed. That's because he operates on a different standard. I could brush my teeth all day long, but if I don't have a way to reach down deep, there will still be problems.

The Bible declares that on even our best days, we've still got stuff between our teeth. Even on our best days, we don't come close to satisfying the demands of a holy God. That's why God's mercy and grace are so important. Until you accept these two things from God in your life, you will delay your destiny and get bogged down in emotions of regret, doubt, shame, and more.

Yet God's mercy through the blood of Christ covers your sins. It covers your past. Your mistakes do not need to keep you from fully living out your destiny. You are bigger than your mistakes. You are a child of the King, fully cleansed by the blood of your loving heavenly Father's perfect sacrifice in His Son.

Is anything in your life keeping you from believing you can live out your destiny? Let it go, and walk confidently in the calling of your King. He has you covered. Learn from your past, but don't live in it. It's a new day, and it's time to move on.

Father, thank You for Your grace and Your mercy. Thank You for covering my sins with the blood of Jesus Christ and for giving me the opportunity to fully live out the plan You have for me.

Running Late

Those who hopefully wait for Me will not be put to shame.

Isaiah 49:23

On one of my speaking trips to Tennessee, my plane was delayed. I got a little nervous because I had to fly to Memphis and then drive an hour to Jackson. I wasn't dressed for the engagement. My clothes were in a garment bag, and I planned on driving to my hotel room and changing before I spoke.

An hour later, we still hadn't boarded. An hour and a half later, we still hadn't boarded. We stayed on the runway for another 30 minutes before we took off. When we finally arrived in Memphis, a man was there to pick me up. I told him I was concerned that we wouldn't have enough time to get to the meeting. He told me not to worry. They would wait.

I told him I was also concerned about having enough time to change my clothes. Again, he told me not worry. He said he'd take me to his father's house, and I could change there.

After driving for an hour, he exited the highway and took me to his father's house to change. I was rushing to change because I hate being late. But the man told me to take my time. He told me the people would wait.

I was feeling frustrated and irritated, trying to rush and get ready. As we left the house, I looked at the clock. We were indeed late for the engagement. The man saw me look at my watch and reminded me yet again not to worry because the people would wait. A few moments later, I walked into a glorious grand ballroom filled with thousands of people. As I entered, they stood up to applaud. They not only waited but even celebrated my arrival.

You may feel like it's taking too long for you to reach your destiny. You may look at your life and think too much time has passed for you to carry out those dreams God put in your heart so long ago. But don't worry—don't be concerned. If you will commit yourself to pursuing God now, your destiny will be there for you according to God's perfect timing. God does not operate on our timetable. Waiting for His perfect timing will not disappoint you. In fact, it will be so wonderful that you may even stand up and applaud.

....

Father, Your timing is different from mine. When I feel like things are late, they are right on time for You. You have a perfect time for everything to take place. I pray that as I wait, I will not complain, but rather look forward to the glorious unfolding of Your perfect plan in my life.

Finishing the Race

Do not fear, for I am with you;
Do not anxiously look about you, for I am your God.
I will strengthen you, surely I will help you,
Surely I will uphold you with My righteous right hand.

ISAIAH 41:10

Derek Redmond was a British sprinter. In the 1992 Olympics in Barcelona, he won his quarter-final heat of the 400. In the semi-final, he started well but tore his hamstring halfway through.

Derek hobbled to a stop and then fell to the track in pain. A stretcher was brought to him, but he was determined to get up and finish the race. Derek's father, Jim Redmond, pushed through security personnel to get to his son. Together, the father and son limped to the finish line as 65,000 spectators stood and cheered.

Something inside us cherishes those moments when people go further than they thought they could. And we wonder, "Would I have the determination to get back up and continue?"

You may have had some bumps and bruises along the path to your destiny. Perhaps you tripped and fell or were knocked down by circumstances out of your control. But I want to remind you that your loving heavenly Father is standing right beside you, ready to help you along. He wants you to finish just as much as you do. And with His help, you can.

Father, thank You for being near me and offering me the help I need to complete my race to fulfill my destiny. Thank You for assisting me and giving me the strength and hope I need to serve You well.

A Reflection of Glory

Everyone who is called by My name,
And whom I have created for My glory,
whom I have formed, even whom I have made.

Isaiah 43:7

One great thing about fulfilling your destiny is getting to share the glory of God. As you live out your destiny, you reflect the glory of God to those around you.

Whatever you think about God, He is much more than that and then some. God displays His glory in creation, but even the universe can't match the glory of God. Keep in mind that the earth makes up only a small portion of creation. God created a universe so big and beautiful and detailed that mankind cannot even comprehend it. In fact, scientists now say the universe is expanding—making it even more difficult to understand its makeup and structure. And God is even more than that.

Everything God created recognizes His glory except for two things: the forces of hell, and mankind. The apostle Paul writes, "Since the creation of the world His invisible attributes, His eternal power and divine nature, have been clearly seen, being understood through what has been made, so that they are without excuse" (Romans 1:20).

Paul also says, "From Him and through Him and to Him are all things. To Him be the glory forever. Amen" (Romans 11:36).

God spoke these words through the prophet Isaiah: "Everyone who is called by My name, and whom I have created for My glory, whom I have formed, even whom I have made" (Isaiah 43:7).

Many people do not know their purpose because they have missed the fundamental premise that life is not about them. It's about Him. God says, "I have created you for My glory." He created you to be the television set or the radio station that transmits the picture and the voice of His invisible attributes. He created you to reflect Him.

As you go about your day—always keep God's glory in the forefront of your mind. If you ever wonder if you're on the right track, ask yourself, "Is what I'm doing reflecting God's glory?" You have been made in the image of God, and His purpose for you is to broadcast that image to those around you.

....

Lord, Your glory is revealed in Your creation. What You have made reflects Your perfection and order. Humanity has only begun to understand a small fraction of how complex the world and universe is, and yet You give me the honor of reflecting Your glory in all that I do. Thank You for this, Lord, and may I do it well.

The Cost of Glory

Then Moses said, "I pray You, show me Your glory."

Exodus 33:18

We glorify God by accomplishing what He tells us to do and not simply what we want to do. Jesus says, "I glorified You on the earth, having accomplished the work which You have given Me to do" (John 17:4). Glorifying God is directly connected to the fulfilling of your destiny. Not every day of your destiny is going to be rainbows and unicorns. Some days will be tough and will require sacrifice.

When God called me to serve the Dallas Cowboys as their chaplain during the height of the Tom Landry years, I gave Him glory by doing the work He had given me to do. But doing that work didn't cost me anything personally. In fact, I was more than happy to do it. I loved that assignment. The tricky part is to give God glory by doing what He has asked you to do when it costs you something, such as your freedom, your personal wants, your comfort, or your pride.

As Jesus was preparing to be taken to the cross and crucified for the sins of all mankind, He said something very revealing about how we are to glorify God. "Now My soul has become troubled; and what shall I say, 'Father, save Me from this hour'? But for this *purpose* I came to this hour. Father, *glorify* Your name" (John 12:27-28).

Jesus didn't mince words or sugarcoat His feelings. His soul was troubled. Jesus wanted to ask God to save Him from this hour. He hoped God would not make Him go through what was about to happen. But then He turned it all around because what He was about to experience was directly tied to His purpose and God's glory. "Go ahead, God," Jesus said, "because this is why I came. Glorify Your name."

Even though Jesus wanted a way out, He finished the work He had been sent to do because He knew that in His purpose—in fulfilling the work God had intended for Him, however painful it was—He was bringing glory to God.

....

Dear God, give me the grace to do the difficult things that come as part of my destiny. Help me to feel Your nearness, especially in those difficult times, so that I will find comfort and strength to endure and fulfill my purpose—all for Your glory.

The Glow of Glory

We all, with unveiled face, beholding as in a mirror the
glory of the Lord, are being transformed into the same image
from glory to glory, just as from the Lord, the Spirit.

2 Corinthians 3:18

Once you view all your life—the good, the bad, and the bitter—through the grid of God's glory, everything changes.

The apostle Paul writes, "We all, with unveiled face, beholding as in a mirror the glory of the Lord, are being transformed into the same image from *glory to glory*, just as from the Lord, the Spirit." Make this decision to unveil your face, heart, and spirit—your soul—before God. Remove the layers of self-preservation, protection, and pride, and authentically trust Him. When you do, you will be transformed. His glory will rest on you and thus become your glory.

You will be like Moses, who was transparent in God's presence for an extended period of time. When he returned to his people, "the sons of Israel would see the face of Moses, that the skin of Moses's face shone" (Exodus 34:35). God's glory was all over Moses. The longer Moses stayed away from God, the more God's glory would fade, and Moses's face would no longer shine as brightly until he returned to God's presence.

God's glory is to radiate inside you so much so that you will have a glow that does not depend on your circumstances. This glow won't have anything to do with your situation. Instead, you will glow because you are embracing God's purpose in your life—to glorify Him by trusting Him even in those situations you cannot understand and do not want to experience.

If you want to know your destiny, live for God's glory even in the daily and mundane things of life (1 Corinthians 10:31). When you live for His glory, He'll reveal your destiny. But He's not going to show it to you if you don't first respect His presence. Once you get that straight, you don't need to knock yourself out trying to track down your destiny. You don't need to go to the ends of the earth to locate your destiny.

Once you determine that you will live for God's glory regardless of what you want to do, feel, or experience, God will bring your destiny to you.

....

Savior, make me a vessel of Your glory by keeping me so close to You that You radiate in me and out of me. I want people to sense Your presence when they come near me—in the words I say and the actions I do.

A Royal Purpose

God is able to make all grace abound to you, so that always having all
sufficiency in everything, you may have an abundance for every good deed.

2 Corinthians 9:8

G od has placed a crown on your head. You are majestic.
Your enemy does not want you to know this. Satan does not
want you to know that you have glory, honor, and dominion from
God.

If Satan can keep you from thinking like royalty, he can keep you
from acting like royalty. If he can convince you that you are nobody,
that you do not matter, and that you have no say, he can trick you
into *acting* as if you are nobody, as if you do not matter, and as if you
have no say.

This is Satan's strategy for preventing you from growing into great-
ness. But I want to let you in on a very powerful secret: You have something that Satan does not.

As a believer in Jesus Christ, you have spiritual authority.

You have been crowned with majesty in God's kingdom. It is up
to you to exercise your royal rights and responsibilities. God alone is
the sovereign and absolute King, but He has given you authority to
accomplish everything you need to do to fulfill your destiny.

God has not only given you spiritual authority, but He has also
empowered you with everything you need to exercise that authority.

If you memorize only one verse in your entire life, memorize this one (it is one of my favorites): "God is able to make all grace abound to you, so that always having all sufficiency in everything, you may have an abundance for every good deed."

What a promise! Anything you do in God's name for His glory—every good deed—is backed by His sufficiency. God doesn't always call the equipped, but He always equips the called. He will equip you to carry out everything He has called you to do. So don't use your own resources to determine whether you can do what God has laid on your heart to do. Instead, look to God and wrap your mind around this verse from 2 Corinthians—and you will experience His power in all you do.

....

Lord, thank You for letting me know that You are there to give me all that I need in order to carry out the tasks You have placed on my heart to perform. That reduces my concern as I look to You to give me the skills and knowledge, the passion and motivation to move forward.

Who Is Calling the Shots?

Behold, I have given you authority to tread on serpents and scorpions,
and over all the power of the enemy, and nothing will injure you.

Luke 10:19

When God sent Moses to Egypt to deliver the Israelites from bondage, He empowered Moses to do the enormous task before him. He said, "See, *I make you as God to Pharaoh*, and your brother Aaron shall be your prophet. You shall speak all that I command you, and your brother Aaron shall speak to Pharaoh that he let the sons of Israel go out of his land" (Exodus 7:1-2).

God told Moses that He was going to make him "as God to Pharaoh" even though everyone thought Pharaoh was running the show. Pharaoh appeared to be in control. He was larger than life and seemed to be calling the shots. Yet God trumps everyone, and when God sends you to do what He has created you to do, He empowers you to do just that. God didn't make Moses *become* God; He made Moses "*as* God to Pharaoh"—meaning He gave Moses authority over the earthly king.

You may face opposition as you live out your destiny. You may have a "Pharaoh" blocking your path. But if you are doing what God has created you to do, you can trust that He has empowered you with all the authority you need.

Keep in mind, though, that God won't force you to live out your purpose, just as He didn't force Moses to confront Pharaoh. That is up to you. Moses could have walked away and said, "You know what, God, that all sounds good, but have You seen Pharaoh? Have You checked out his army? I appreciate the vote of confidence, God…but get real!" Moses could have said all of those things and left. And as a result, we would be reading about someone else in the Scripture whom God used to set His people free.

Unfortunately, many of us have given away our destiny by forfeiting our spiritual authority. Sometimes Satan doesn't even have to fight for it. Have you ever examined your situation, seen the size of the challenge, looked at your own inadequacies…and given up? When we do that, we hand over to Satan the authority God intends for us to use.

Fortunately, you can get it back. You can be fully empowered to live out your complete, God-given potential. You can reclaim your spiritual authority. Just place your faith in God and do what He asks you to do.

....

Dear God, I want to fully live out the spiritual authority You have given me. I pray for wisdom to know how to exercise authority in my daily life on the journey toward my destiny.

The One Thing

Call to Me and I will answer you, and I will tell you
great and mighty things, which you do not know.

Jeremiah 33:3

One day a man visited his doctor because he was in excruciating pain. The doctor asked him, "Where does it hurt?"

"All over," the man answered.

The doctor told the man to touch his shoulder. The man touched his shoulder and cried out in pain. Next, the doctor told the man to touch his forehead. The man touched his forehead and cried out in pain again. The doctor told the man to touch his knee. The man touched his knee and winced in pain. He said, "Doctor, everywhere I touch, I'm in pain."

The doctor thoroughly examined the man and concluded, "No wonder you are in pain everywhere you touch—you have a dislocated finger!"

We may laugh at the man's ridiculous situation, but many of us do the same thing in a different way. We feel like everything in our lives is wrong, yet in fact just one thing is wrong—and that one thing affects everything. This one thing is that many of us are living a life without purpose. We are simply going through the motions—existing day by day, weighed down by the emptiness of a life without meaning.

Purpose is not measured by comparing what you have done to

what someone else has done but by comparing what you have done to what you are supposed to do. The only way to know your purpose is to experience and walk closely with the One who has created and destined you for it. If you are a Christian, you do not need to try to discover your purpose. Rather, it is in experiencing God that your purpose will be made known. Experience God, and you will experience your purpose. Know God, and you will know your destiny.

....

I call to You, Father, and ask that You will answer me. I ask that You will show me the great and mighty things that I do not yet know. Mark my steps according to Your divine will for my life.

Seeking Without Striving

Cease striving and know that I am God;
I will be exalted among the nations,
I will be exalted in the earth.

PSALM 46:10

One of the greatest benefits that arises out of a close relationship with our heavenly Father is that He will guide, direct, and prepare us to experience the purpose He has for our lives. When you truly embrace the principle expressed in the verse above, you will experience the abundant joy that Christ has promised you. You will no longer be straining and striving to see if this plan will work, or if this relationship will work, or if this job will work, or if this path will work. When you *know* that God is God—and you seek to get close to Him—He will show you your path and your purpose.

If you want to experience God's purpose for your life, experience God. Don't go looking for His will; look for Him. In close, abiding intimacy with the Father, you will discover and live out the destiny He has purposed for you. When you seek Him first, God takes responsibility to provide all you need for whatever He wants you to do (Matthew 6:33). You won't have to break your neck to get it. You won't have to wear yourself out trying to accomplish it. God will flow it naturally to you because, after all, He will receive the glory. God doesn't mind picking up the tab to bring your destiny your way when He knows that you will do it no matter what and He will get the glory.

As you continue this journey of destiny, you have a daily decision to make. For whose glory will you live? Will you live for your name, your reputation, your recognition, your exaltation, and your 15 minutes of fame? Because if that's what you want, that's what you'll get, and trust me—15 minutes of fame is still only 15 minutes in light of eternity. It's not going to last that long.

Or are you going to live for the eternal King, who rules over an eternal kingdom? His destiny for you includes and benefits you, but it has been designed to advance His kingdom on earth, bless others, and reflect His greatest glory.

....

Lord, I rest in Your presence as I make You the highest priority in my life. As I choose each day to do this one thing—to put You first—I know that You will always provide what I need to carry out my purpose.

A Big Little Word

In all these things we overwhelmingly conquer through Him who loved us.

ROMANS 8:37

You exist for God. You are His special creation. He formed you and He made you because He loves you. You have a reason to get up every morning: to fulfill the purpose God has for your life. And it is a great purpose, a wonderful purpose. In fact, God tells you in Jeremiah 29:11 that He has a good plan for you when you seek Him and His will for your life. You've heard it before, but let this sink in: God has a good plan just for you.

The God who created you for Himself has never made a mistake. His plan for you has no failures or flaws. Yes, you will have to endure trials, but they will work together for good if you love God, draw near to God...experience God. He promises.

God's Word tells us, "In all these things [trials, struggles, emptiness, pain...] we overwhelmingly conquer through Him who loved us" (Romans 8:37). Do you know something? The most important word in that verse is often overlooked. I must have preached on that verse 100 times in the past 30 years, but I never saw it until just this month. I was studying this passage in relation to my own life, and I felt as if God took a yellow highlighter and made this word come alive.

You might be thinking "conquer" or "overwhelmingly" is the most important word in that verse. Actually, no. The most important word is "in."

We are often tempted to believe that God has promised to keep us "from" trials, tests, and pains, and then when He doesn't, we feel let down, discouraged, or defeated. But God never promised to deliver us *from* all things. He has promised that "*in* all these things" we will overwhelmingly conquer. We will experience Him. We will receive the benefits and blessings that come because of our deep and meaningful experience of Him.

Thank You, God, for being with me in all things and giving me Your strength to overwhelmingly conquer. Thank You that I need not fear, doubt, or worry, because the God who holds the universe in place holds me together as well.

Baggage

*You shall love the LORD your God with all your heart
and with all your soul and with all your might.*

DEUTERONOMY 6:5

A couple planned an elaborate summer vacation in Europe. They packed their bags for two months of fun, rest, and relaxation. When the ticket agent asked how many bags they were checking the husband said to his wife, "Dear, I wish we would have brought the piano."

Confused, she asked why they needed to bring the piano.

"Because I left the tickets and itinerary on the piano," he replied.

Many of us are carrying a lot of baggage in our lives. Pain, problems, frustrations, failures…if we transport these things into our future, they can prevent us from fully living out our destinies.

In your daily walk with God and the fulfillment of your purpose, consider lightening your load so you can focus on the main thing. Jesus told His disciples in Matthew 6:33, "Seek first His kingdom and His righteousness, and all these things will be added to you." When we focus on anything other than God's kingdom and righteousness, we can become worried, insecure, and anxious. The enemy uses those distractions to get us off track from fulfilling our divine reason for being—our destiny.

When we put our relationship with God on the front burner of our lives rather than the back burner, we experience God's power and provision at a level that far exceeds what we could ever manufacture on our own. We live out the victory that is ours to enjoy. And we will reach the end of our lives knowing that we have truly fulfilled our destiny.

Lord, I want to love You with all my heart, with all my soul, with all my mind, and with all my strength. Reveal to me the areas in my life where I am not doing this, and give me the wisdom to know how to change.

Trading Yesterday for Tomorrow

Let us fear if, while a promise remains of entering His
rest, any one of you may seem to have come short of it.

Hebrews 4:1

D o you remember Jed Clampett and *The Beverly Hillbillies*? What
made that show so funny was that Jed and his crew had been delivered from their old life in the middle of nowhere, but they were still
living as hillbillies in their new life in Beverly Hills. Their location had
changed, but their mindset hadn't.

The same was true for the Israelites who escaped Egypt after 430
years of oppression. The Israelites had left Egypt, but Egypt had not
left them. Having traveled to the Promised Land and sent spies to
examine it, they stood on the precipice of a glorious tomorrow. But
instead of trusting God to give them their inheritance, they chose to
focus on the challenges they would face. Rather than celebrating, they
grumbled and complained. They even wanted to go back to their past
instead of continuing into their future.

When God delivered the Israelites from Egypt, He did not
only deliver them from their past, He also delivered them *to* their
future—Canaan. Yet because they chose to be so focused on yesterday, they missed their tomorrow. As a result, they were forced to wan-
der in the wilderness for 40 years so God could disconnect them from
their past.

Many of us cannot get excited about tomorrow because we are still clinging to our past. We cannot step into our future because we cannot even get through today. The Israelites were tethered to their past because they failed to do what Hebrews chapter 4 tells us is essential: to combine God's word with faith. We read, "Therefore, let us fear if, while a promise remains of entering His rest, any one of you may seem to have come short of it. For indeed we have had good news preached to us, just as they also; but the word they heard did not profit them, because it was not united by faith in those who heard" (Hebrews 4:1-2).

To have faith is to act on God's Word. Having faith is acting like something *is* so even when it is *not* so in order for it to *be* so simply because God *said* so. Faith is always an action. That is why we are told to "walk by faith" rather than being told to "talk by faith." Until we actively apply God's Word to our lives, it remains a spiritual theory. It will not become a concrete experience. Without an action, it will die in the wilderness. God is not as interested in your "amen" as He is in your action as you live out your destiny.

....

Lord, make me a person of active faith—acting in a way that reveals my confidence in You and Your Word.

Watch Where You're Going

Sanctify them in the truth; Your word is truth.

JOHN 17:17

If you want a bag of cement to become concrete, you must mix it with water. Likewise, you must mix God's Word with faith in order for it to become a concrete experience in your life.

The walk from Egypt to Canaan should have taken the people of Israel about 35 days, but it took them 40 years because they kept looking back. Maybe that sounds familiar to you. Maybe you feel that you should have been further in your life by now, further in your career, your relationships, your family, your finances, or your emotional and spiritual well-being, but instead you keep looking back. You keep saying "what if" and "why" and "if only."

You fear that you have blown it. You have missed your opportunity. You have failed. Or you fear that someone else has messed you up too much, ruined your future, or stolen your hope. Yesterday is real—there is no denying that. But you don't have to keep looking back like the Israelites did: "We remember the fish which we used to eat free in Egypt, the cucumbers and the melons and the leeks" (Numbers 11:5). Instead, you can look at the milk and honey of your destiny. God promised the Israelites a bountiful tomorrow, just as He promises you a wonderful destiny. As His child, you have a future filled with hope.

Never underestimate God. He can turn a mess into a miracle. That's what He did in the lives of Moses, Rahab, Sarah, Peter, Jacob, and so many others in Scripture. Let their lives serve as testimonies to what God can and will do through you…if you will put your hope and trust in Him. The next time you feel like complaining, praise Him instead. Don't praise Him for the mess or for the pain; praise Him that He is bigger than the mess and the pain and that He can sanctify all of it, setting you on the path of purpose.

Dear God, thank You for this reminder to look forward and not backward. I want to move ahead and fully live on purpose, so I choose to let go of the past and embrace all You have in store for me now.

The Final Word

*[You] have been buried with Him in baptism, in which
you were also raised up with Him through faith in the
working of God, who raised Him from the dead.*

COLOSSIANS 2:12

Do you want to know the secret to victoriously living out your destiny? Would you like to know how to defeat Satan in every battle he brings against you? The secret lies in your union with Jesus Christ.

The book of Colossians tells us that we have "been made complete, and He is the head over all rule and authority" (Colossians 2:10). Jesus is the head. That means that He is in charge over all power and authority. He has the ultimate say over Satan. He has the final word.

Your challenge may have *a* word, or your boss may have *a* word, or your crisis may have *a* word, or that relationship may have *a* word...but these things do not have the *final* word. If something is holding you down and keeping you from fully living out your destiny, remember that it does not have the final word. Jesus is the head over all power and authority. Jesus has the final word over everything.

We also read in Colossians that you have received the fullness of Christ, in whom is "all the fullness of Deity" (Colossians 2:9). In other words, everything that God is, His complete essence, dwells in Jesus Christ. And everything that makes up Christ, including His position as head over all power and authority, dwells in you.

The closer you abide with Christ, the closer you are to living out your purpose. Everything you need is found in Him. So spend time with Jesus. Abide with Him. Talk to Him on a regular basis. Make knowing Him an important part of all that you do. He will guide you and direct you and make your path clear to you. Not only that, but He will cover you and protect you when you need it the most.

....

Jesus, I want to know You more. I want to sense Your presence and have Your thoughts guide my own. Help me to cultivate my relationship with You every day.

Resolutions

Surely goodness and lovingkindness will follow me all the days of my life,
And I will dwell in the house of the LORD forever.

PSALM 23:6

Many of us make New Year's resolutions, and most of us break them. They may include being a better person, eating healthier, working out at the gym, memorizing Scripture, or watching fewer football games. A resolution is simply a firm decision to do something. It's a decree or promise.

Every January, our resolutions resound with determination and the hope of new beginnings. By May, their nagging presence reminds us that we didn't quite reach our goals. By December, most of us have forgotten what we had resolved to do.

Regardless of whether you join with the millions in making New Year's resolutions, I want to remind you that there is One who has kept every resolution He has ever made. He keeps His promises. He keeps His Word.

And even if we are not able to stick it out in the gym, stay away from the chocolate, or bite our tongue rather than beat others with it, He is able to do exceedingly, abundantly above all we could ever imagine. And He has resolved that your life is going to be a *great* life as you live out your purpose. It is a life filled with "a future and a hope." The surest way to live out your destiny is to fix your eyes on the unchanging faithfulness of the One who has promised that goodness and loving-kindness will follow you when you follow Him.

....

My God, guide me that I may walk in the steps You have for me. I know that in following You I will experience the goodness and loving-kindness You have in store for me as I live out my perfect destiny.

Lessons in the Dark

So will My word be which goes forth from My mouth;
It will not return to Me empty,
Without accomplishing what I desire,
And without succeeding in the matter for which I sent it.

ISAIAH 55:11

Your life may hold some surprises, but I know who holds your life. And He says that you are to be of good cheer, because He has already overcome all of them. If He has overcome them, then you have overcome them too as His child and as His heir.

I understand how easily we can get caught up in the circumstances of life. Things can seem overwhelming. I understand how easily we can lose hope. But if you will keep your eyes fixed on the Lord and not on your circumstances, you will see that He who began a good work in you will also complete it.

People lose hope when they can't see a future. Yesterday was bleak, today is still bleak, and tomorrow doesn't look any better. The weather report of their lives says, "No sunshine." Nothing out there has their number on it or seems related to their calling or destiny.

But when God says He has a plan, you know the story isn't over. In fact, you are still here, so your life is not over. Your destiny is not over. Your purpose is not over. Your calling is not over. If you are still living, breathing, and functioning on planet Earth, God has a plan just for you.

You may be saying, "But, Tony, you don't know about my past. It's messed up—God would never use me." Well, Israel had a past too. Yet God still had a plan for them that included a future and a hope. Remember, some of your greatest lessons about faith and humility will be learned in the dark. These are the times when you feel so hopeless that you don't know what in the world God is doing, how He is doing it, and why He is taking so long.

God may be silent, but He is not still. When you feel furthest from Him, He is the closest He'll ever be. One of the key components of a life of destiny is to trust in the Lord in times that don't make sense.

Thank You, God, for giving me hope amid trials and stress. When I look back at some of the mistakes in my life, I wonder how the plans ahead could be so good. But You have a good plan for me, and I'm grateful You will carry it out.

Seize the Moment

Seek the welfare of the city where I have sent you into exile, and pray to the LORD on its behalf; for in its welfare you will have welfare.

JEREMIAH 29:7

Waiting on the timing of your destiny is not the same thing as sitting back and doing nothing. God says to become as productive as you possibly can where you are. Do all that is in your hand to do. Maximize everything that is set before you. Seize the moment right where you are. While waiting on God for your destiny, promote the well-being of the people around you now. Even if you are not where you want to be or if you are not doing what you want to do, benefit those around you. Invest in them and increase the well-being of their lives.

Surely the Israelites were not happy about their captivity in Babylon, but God instructed them to pray for the Babylonians and to work for their betterment. He told them that in the Babylonians' well-being, they would find their own. God would bless them for being a blessing to others.

Many of us choose to do nothing while waiting on God to bring about change in our lives or get us out of difficult situations. But the only time you are to do nothing is when there is nothing to do. If there is nothing you can do, then do nothing. But if God has given you something to do where you are right now, do it with all your might.

Invest in your surroundings right now. Seek the well-being of those around you. As you become a blessing to others, you set yourself up to be blessed. As you help others locate and live out their destinies, you set yourself up to discover your own.

....

I want to help others pursue their destinies, Lord, even as I live out my own. Open my eyes to see how I can be a blessing to those around me, in Your name.

Comfort in Your Pain

Blessed be the God and Father of our Lord Jesus Christ,
the Father of mercies and God of all comfort.

2 Corinthians 1:3

I wish I could tell you in good conscience that if you come to Jesus, it won't rain on your parade or that you will no longer experience difficulties, trials, delays, or disappointments. If I could tell you that, I imagine you might shout, clap your hands, and wear a big smile. I would too.

But I can't tell you that, simply because it's not true. Yet what I *can* tell you ought to paint a smile on your face, because when you fully grasp this, it will change the way you view life's pain. Here it is: God never allows anything in your life that He does not simultaneously promise to use for good if you are one of His children and living according to His purpose.

If you will make Jesus your focus, He will make His love your comfort and your strength. Place your eyes on Him because He is *for* you. Paul reminds us of the comfort we have as children of God: "Blessed be the God and Father of our Lord Jesus Christ, the Father of mercies and God of all comfort, who comforts us in all our affliction" (2 Corinthians 1:3-4). Jesus also assures us that He has asked His Father to send us the comfort we need: "I will ask the Father, and He will give you another Helper, that He may be with you forever" (John 14:16).

So I can't say to you that if you come to Jesus or focus on Him, it will never rain. What I *can* say to you is that if you will keep your eyes on Him and His promises in His Word, then when the storms come, He will be your covering. He will be your umbrella. He will be the shelter that guards your emotions, your dreams, and the deepest part of who you are. He will protect and nurture that tender part of you that we often refer to as the core or spirit. It is the truest and most authentic version of yourself.

Jesus will not only cover you but also use the trials and troubles of this life to guide you into the fullest realization of your destiny.

Lord, pain is real. I can feel it, and I don't always like it. In times of pain, I sometimes forget about pursuing my destiny because I'm so focused on myself and trying to find relief. Please help me to remember that You have a purpose in the pain and that You can use it for good if I will cooperate with You in it.

Never Alone

Even though I walk through the valley of the shadow of death,
I fear no evil, for You are with me;
Your rod and Your staff, they comfort me.

Psalm 23:4

God longs for a deep and abiding relationship with you. Because He is dependable, He wants you to depend on Him.

If you are healthy, you aren't likely to be going to the doctor's office anytime soon. This is because everything in your body seems to be working and doing what it is supposed to do. But when you become sick, and especially if that sickness continues for a long time, chances are that you will make an appointment to go visit your doctor.

Similarly, sometimes God allows troubles or trials in your life to get your focus back onto Him and the purpose He has for you. He doesn't want you to walk this road alone. He is with you even when you forget that He's there. He longs to be close to you. His power and grace are with you, and they will comfort and direct you.

God sometimes calls us to walk through valleys. I can't promise you that life will be without wind, clouds, and rain. But I *can* promise you that you don't have to walk through the valley alone. If you will cast your eyes on Jesus Christ, He will meet you where you are. So keep walking. Don't throw in the towel.

Don't say that you can't make it, because God will make it with you. You don't walk the road of destiny all alone.

....

Dear God, thank You for being so close to me that in the valleys of my life, I am not alone. Thank You for bringing comfort when I need it and using the trials of life to guide me along the path of my destiny.

Experiencing Faith

Truly I say to you, if you have faith the size of a mustard seed, you will say to this mountain, "Move from here to there," and it will move; and nothing will be impossible to you.

MATTHEW 17:20

Faith is not measured by how much you believe in what you believe. Faith is about believing that the One you believe in is believable. In fact, you can have all the faith in the world that your SUV is going to take off and fly you to Canada at 12,000 feet, but you'll still be stuck in traffic with all four wheels firmly on the ground.

How can you find out whether the One you believe in is believable? By knowing and experiencing Him.

Picture a child climbing up on her daddy's back for a piggyback ride. She doesn't ask herself whether he can hold her or if he is going to drop her. She simply asks, "Do you have me?" as she wiggles and adjusts her legs into place.

By asking her daddy, "Do you have me?" she is affirming her confidence that he is trustworthy. When he says, "Yes, I have you" and they enjoy a safe ride, she will have even more confidence in him the next time.

But what if she is unsure her daddy will keep her safe? She can say all day long that she believes he can carry her, but saying it a thousand times won't reduce the hesitation she feels. She will never experience the full pleasure of his presence until she takes that first climb of faith and discovers that he is more than able to support her.

Faith becomes real when it is experienced. Saying you believe God has you on your path of destiny is easy. Feeling like you believe is also easy. But faith is not based on your feelings. Faith is experienced in your feet. That's why the Bible calls it "walking by faith" rather than "feeling by faith."

Demonstrate your faith by taking action to live out your destiny. Take God seriously. Hold Him accountable to His Word. Discover all the promises He has in store for you, and then receive them by believing that what God says is true.

Dear God, increase my faith so I can see mountains move. Make me an instrument of faith that reflects Your truth as I journey toward the fulfillment of my destiny.

The Treasure

*The kingdom of heaven is like a treasure hidden in the
field, which a man found and hid again; and from joy over
it he goes and sells all that he has and buys that field.*

MATTHEW 13:44

I love action-adventure movies that feature brave protagonists searching for something valuable. I love to watch these characters persevere through a long, involved pursuit of their goal. Of course, they
face unimaginable danger along the way—obstacles to overcome and
enemies to defeat. Yet the heroes always make it. And in the end, they
always uncover the treasure.

Jesus speaks of a treasure—the kingdom of God. He says that this
kingdom is unusually valuable and that absolutely nothing should
stand in the way of claiming it. Eschatologically, the kingdom will be
consummated in the millennial reign of Christ, when He will return
to the earth to rule from Jerusalem for a thousand years. Yet we have
begun to experience the kingdom here and now—its principles, cov-
enants, responsibilities, privileges, rights, rules, ethics, covering, and
authority.

A priceless treasure like this is worth fighting for. It is worth everything you have. But don't just take my word for it. Jesus said it Himself.

Many of us today are living without the thrill of finding a hidden
treasure. We have not understood the mystery of the kingdom, settling

instead for trinkets, gadgets, sports, entertainment, shopping, careers, and vacations.

And those things are okay…unless they distract you from pursuing the kingdom. They can be wonderful blessings, but they must not become your goal. The fullest expression of your destiny will always be tied to the treasure of the kingdom. Pursue this treasure, and you will discover a life well lived.

....

Father, I pray that Your kingdom will be advanced on earth and that Your glory will fill the earth. May I be a part of making this happen. Use me in Your kingdom work, and I will be forever grateful.

Behind the Scenes

Many plans are in a man's heart,
But the counsel of the LORD will stand.

PROVERBS 19:21

God has a plan for you. He has a destiny for you. Maybe you should have gotten it earlier in your life. Maybe you shouldn't have done this, that, or the other thing that got you off track. Or maybe if someone else wouldn't have done something to you, you would have gotten it earlier. Maybe if you had gotten saved earlier, hadn't married that person out of God's will, hadn't sought a career out of His will, or hadn't just been plain rebellious, maybe you would have reached your destiny earlier. Regardless, God has a plan for you. And it's a good plan, filled with a future and a hope.

Israel would not see God's plan fulfilled for 70 years. The prophets were falsely telling them about their deliverance (Jeremiah 14:14; 29:8-9). But the prophets didn't know what they were talking about. They just said whatever the people wanted to hear. God knew the exile would last longer than they thought. That's why He told them to be as productive as they could be right where they were until they saw Him do what He said He would do.

The Israelites didn't like being in bondage, and I'm sure you don't like being in the dark about your destiny. Your best course of action is to seek God. "Without faith it is impossible to please Him, for he who comes to God must believe that He is and that He is a rewarder of those who seek Him" (Hebrews 11:6). If you don't know which way to go, seek Him. If you are in pain, seek Him. If you are confused, seek Him. If you are waiting, seek Him. You need to seek Him to discover your destiny.

Sometimes God will seem to be doing nothing. Yet He often works invisibly—behind the scenes—by turning yesterday's pains into tomorrow's peace. God is asking you to take hold of His hand and never let go because He knows where He is taking you. It is a good, wonderful place because it has a future and a hope. What God starts, God finishes. What God begins, God ends. What God initiates, God completes.

....

Dear God, I know You have a perfect plan for me, and I'm excited to live it out. Thank You for revealing as much as You have so far, and please lead me into the fullness of Your plan so I may fulfill Your calling on my life.

The Central Theme of the Bible

The kingdom of God is not eating and drinking, but
righteousness and peace and joy in the Holy Spirit.

ROMANS 14:17

The Bible is not an anthology of random stories. The thread that ties the entire Bible together is the theme of the kingdom. God's goal is for His rule and authority to cover the earth through the expansion of His kingdom. That is God's purpose in history.

Scripture was penned to facilitate that one agenda. The unifying central theme of the Bible is the glory of God through the advancement of His kingdom. Every event, story, and personality, from Genesis to Revelation, is there to stitch that theme together. Without that theme, the Bible becomes a collection of disconnected stories that seem to be unrelated to each other.

Similarly, when you do not recognize and incorporate the theme of the kingdom in your own life, your experiences will likewise seem disconnected, unrelated, and random. They will lack the cohesion that your destiny provides. Understanding and embracing God's kingdom is the secret to living with meaning, simply because your life is tied to His kingdom. God's kingdom agenda for you and for all others is based on His comprehensive rule over every area of life.

We celebrate our country and our citizenship by reciting the Pledge of Allegiance and singing the national anthem. But if you have been born again through Jesus Christ, you are part of an even greater kingdom. You are a citizen of the kingdom of God.

Understanding what the kingdom is and how it impacts you is vitally important because it explains your life and purpose. It shows you how things blend together to create an integrated whole. It gives your life meaning. Apart from the kingdom, the events and aspects of your life remain unattached to each other and cannot produce their intended results.

....

Thank You for Your kingdom, Lord. May Your kingdom be advanced on earth and may Your will be done on earth as it is in heaven.

Expectations

When the Son of Man comes in His glory, and all the angels
with Him, then He will sit on His glorious throne.

MATTHEW 25:31

Your expectations always affect your behavior. If you found out you were terminally ill and had only one year to live, I can guarantee you would rethink your choices. If you suddenly knew you would be gone in 12 months, certain things that used to be important wouldn't be important anymore. You would want to right certain wrongs because your expectation of death would transform the way you function in life.

The Bible refers to the return of Jesus Christ as the blessed hope (Titus 2:13). It is the great expectation of the church that time is not all there is, that eternity awaits us, and that God will lead us there.

I believe many believers aren't living a life of purpose because they've lost that blessed expectation. Maybe you're a bit like that. You may have lost sight of the prophetic Word of God, and as a result, you've lost direction and momentum in your daily life and your walk of faith. Choose to draw near to God again through His prophetic Word.

We study eschatology, or end-times prophecy, so we can learn how to function while we await Christ's return. As a member of the body of Christ, you are to provide a glimpse of eternity by fulfilling your destiny. You are a preview of the coming attraction! As you put your faith in God's Word, you are bringing a little bit of heaven to the world around you while you wait for God's kingdom to fill the earth.

....

Lord, I want to live in the light of Your prophetic Word and Your coming kingdom. Teach me how to live my life and fulfill my purpose in a way that advances Your overarching plan.

Bearing Fruit for a Purpose

Delight yourself in the LORD,
And He will give you the desires of your heart.

PSALM 37:4

Look carefully at the structure of today's verse. It implies an "if-then" construction: *If* you delight yourself in the Lord, *then* He will give you the desires of your heart. When you delight yourself in the Lord, His agenda becomes your own. His priorities outrank yours. You judge the importance of things by His standard.

A person who is delighted in the Lord may very well desire a house or a car or some other nice thing. But they will pray, "Lord, give me this thing so it can become Yours. Meet my need so I can advance Your kingdom." It is as though God is saying, "If you want My blessings so you can build a kingdom of your own, don't expect much. I'm only interested in answering the prayers of people who are serious about being fruitful for My kingdom."

As we read in the book of John, "My Father is glorified by this, that you bear much fruit, and so prove to be My disciples" (John 15:8). As with every other facet of our lives, we bear fruit to glorify God. In fact, the entire universe exists to glorify God. You and I find our place in the universe by understanding and participating in that divine purpose. The more fruitful we grow, the better we reflect the glory of God and the less we muddy the waters with our own shortsighted agendas.

Many of the world's observatories still use giant reflecting telescopes. They work on a simple principle: An enormous curved mirror gathers faint light from distant stars and reflects it onto a small eyepiece. The reflecting power of the mirror enables astronomers to view the wonders of space.

Our fruit reflects God's glory and enables us to focus His light on our dark, needy world. Your purpose is to glorify God by bearing fruit in His name for your good and the betterment of others.

Lord, I delight myself in You. I want the things that bring You joy and happiness to bring me joy and happiness as well. Thank You for being so clear about my greatest purpose in life—to bear fruit for Your glory and Your kingdom agenda.

The Power of Thanks

Your kingdom come.
Your will be done,
On earth as it is in heaven.

MATTHEW 6:10

The gift of life cannot be fully enjoyed until it is given and received as a gift. Some people act as though they could snatch life from God's hands or steal it while He isn't looking. They don't want the gift; they want ownership. But God can't be fooled. He wants to give us life and to stay in our lives as an essential part of the gift. He also wants us to be thankful for the life He gives. We can refuse the gift if we don't like the terms, but there are no other terms on which we can beg, borrow, steal, or buy the abundant life Jesus came to give. Mere existence is the only alternative.

If you have accepted the gift of life, how does God know you are thankful? Going to church on Sunday is only a small part of it because God is just as interested in the rest of your week.

You demonstrate your thankfulness by letting Him run your life.

Think for a moment about the model for prayer that Jesus gave to His disciples in Matthew 6. He prayed, "Your will be done, on earth as it is in heaven." How is God's will enacted in heaven? Completely. Perfectly. Absolutely. In heaven, everybody and everything conforms to the will of God. His will is everything—there is no other option.

As you live out your destiny, God wants you to be so grateful to Him for His gift of life and His provision that you surrender your life to Him. When you give your life back to Him, He can give the greatest gift of all—the abundance found in living out your purpose. Nothing short of that will do.

Surrender is the key to your destiny. It is the thing that will unlock all that God has in store for you. Surrender, and then hold on for the ride of your life! It's going to be awesome.

Father in heaven, hallowed be Your name. Your kingdom come, and Your will be done on earth as it is in heaven. And begin, Lord, with me.

Dr. Tony Evans and
The Urban Alternative

About Dr. Tony Evans

Dr. Tony Evans is founder and senior pastor of the 10,000-member Oak Cliff Bible Fellowship in Dallas, founder and president of the Urban Alternative, chaplain of the NBA's Dallas Mavericks, and author of many books, including *Destiny* and *Victory in Spiritual Warfare*. His radio broadcast, *The Alternative with Dr. Tony Evans*, can be heard on more than 1,000 outlets and in more than 100 countries.

The Urban Alternative

The Urban Alternative (TUA) equips, empowers, and unites Christians to impact individuals, families, churches, and communities through a thoroughly kingdom agenda worldview. In teaching truth, we seek to transform lives.

The core cause of the problems we face in our personal lives, homes, churches, and societies is spiritual; therefore, the only way to address it is spiritually. We've tried a political, social, economic, and even a religious agenda. It's time for a kingdom agenda—the visible manifestation of the comprehensive rule of God over every area of life.

The unifying, central theme of the Bible is the glory of God and the advancement of His kingdom. This is the conjoining thread from Genesis to Revelation—from beginning to end. Without that theme, the Bible might look like disconnected stories that are inspiring but seem to be unrelated in purpose and direction. The Bible exists to share God's movement in history to establish and expand His kingdom. Understanding that increases the relevance of these ancient writings in our day-to-day living because the kingdom is not only then—it is now.

The absence of the kingdom's influence in our own lives and in our families, churches, and communities has led to a catastrophic deterioration in our world.

- People live segmented, compartmentalized lives because they lack God's kingdom worldview.

- Families disintegrate because they exist for their own satisfaction rather than for the kingdom.

- Churches have limited impact because they fail to comprehend that the goal of the church is not to advance the church itself, but the kingdom.

- Communities have nowhere to turn to find real solutions for real people who have real problems, because the church has become divided, ingrown, and powerless to transform the cultural landscape in any relevant way.

The kingdom agenda offers us a way to live with a solid hope by optimizing the solutions of heaven. When God and His rule are not the final and authoritative standard over all, order and hope are lost. But the reverse of that is true as well—as long as we have God, we have hope. If God is still in the picture, and as long as His agenda is still on the table, it's not over.

Even if relationships collapse, God will sustain you. Even if finances dwindle, God will keep you. Even if dreams die, God will revive you. As long as God and His rule guide your life, family, church, and community, there is always hope.

Our world needs the King's agenda. Our churches need the King's agenda. Our families need the King's agenda.

In many major cities, drivers can take a loop to get to the other side of the city without driving straight through downtown. This loop takes them close enough to the city to see its towering buildings and skyline, but not close enough to actually experience it.

This is precisely what our culture has done with God. We have put Him on the "loop" of our personal, family, church, and community lives. He's close enough to be at hand should we need Him in an emergency, but far enough away that He can't be the center of who we are.

Sadly, we often want God on the loop of our lives, but we don't always want the King of the Bible to come downtown into the very heart of our ways. Leaving God on the loop brings about dire consequences, as we have seen in our own lives and with others. But when we make God and His rule the centerpiece of all we think, do, and say, we experience Him in the way He longs for us to.

He wants us to be kingdom people with kingdom minds set on fulfilling His kingdom purposes. He wants us to pray as Jesus did—"Not my will, but Yours be done" (Luke 22:42)—because His is the kingdom, the power, and the glory.

There is only one God, and we are not Him. As King and Creator, God calls the shots. Only when we align ourselves underneath His comprehensive authority will we access His full power and authority in our lives, families, churches, and communities.

As we learn how to govern ourselves under God, we will transform the institutions of family, church, and society according to a biblically based, kingdom worldview. Under Him, we touch heaven and change earth.

To achieve our goal, we use a variety of strategies, approaches, and resources for reaching and equipping as many people as possible.

Broadcast Media

Millions of individuals experience *The Alternative with Dr. Tony Evans*, a daily broadcast playing on nearly 1,000 radio outlets and in more than 100 countries. The broadcast can also be seen on several television networks, online at TonyEvans.org, and on the free Tony

Evans app. More than four million message downloads occur each year.

Leadership Training

The *Tony Evans Training Center (TETC)* facilitates educational programming that embodies the ministry philosophy of Dr. Tony Evans as expressed through the kingdom agenda. The training courses focus on leadership development and discipleship in five tracks:

- Bible and theology
- personal growth
- family and relationships
- church health and leadership development
- society and community impact

The TETC program includes courses for both local and online students. Furthermore, TETC programming includes course work for nonstudent attendees. Pastors, Christian leaders, and Christian laity, both local and at a distance, can seek the Kingdom Agenda Certificate for personal, spiritual, and professional development. Some courses qualify for continuing education credits and will transfer for college credit with our partner schools.

Kingdom Agenda Pastors (KAP) provides a viable network for like-minded pastors who embrace the kingdom agenda philosophy. Pastors have the opportunity to go deeper with Dr. Tony Evans as they are given greater biblical knowledge, practical applications, and resources to impact individuals, families, churches, and communities. KAP welcomes senior and associate pastors of all churches. KAP also offers an annual summit, held each year in Dallas, Texas, with intensive seminars, workshops, and resources.

Pastors' Wives Ministry, founded by Dr. Lois Evans, provides counsel, encouragement, and spiritual resources for pastors' wives as they serve with their husbands in ministry. A primary focus of the ministry is the KAP Summit, which offers senior pastors' wives a safe place to reflect, renew, and relax along with training in personal development, spiritual growth, and care for their emotional and physical well-being.

Community Impact

National Church Adopt-A-School Initiative (NCAASI) empowers churches across the country to impact communities through public schools, effecting positive social change in urban youth and families. Leaders of churches, school districts, faith-based organizations, and other nonprofit organizations are equipped with the knowledge and tools to forge partnerships and build strong social service delivery systems. This training is based on the comprehensive church-based community impact strategy conducted by Oak Cliff Bible Fellowship. It addresses areas such as economic development, education, housing, health revitalization, family renewal, and racial reconciliation. NCAASI assists churches in tailoring the model to meet specific needs of their communities, while addressing the spiritual and moral frame of reference. Training events are held annually in the Dallas area at Oak Cliff Bible Fellowship.

Athlete's Impact (AI) is an outreach into and through sports. Coaches are sometimes the most influential adults in young people's lives—even more than parents. With the rise of fatherlessness in our culture, more young people are looking to their coaches for guidance, character development, practical needs, and hope. Athletes (professional or amateur) also influence younger athletes and kids. Knowing this, we equip and train coaches and athletes to live out and utilize their God-given roles for the benefit of the kingdom. We aim to do this through our iCoach App, weCoach Football Conference, and other resources, such as *The Playbook: A Life Strategy Guide for Athletes.*

Resource Development

We foster lifelong learning partnerships with the people we serve by providing a variety of published materials. Dr. Evans has published more than 100 unique titles (booklets, books, and Bible studies) based on more than 40 years of preaching. Our goal is to strengthen individuals in their walk with God and service to others.

For more information and a complimentary copy of Dr. Evans's devotional newsletter,

call
(800) 800-3222

or write
TUA
PO Box 4000
Dallas TX 75208

or visit
www.TonyEvans.org

MORE GREAT
HARVEST HOUSE BOOKS
BY DR. TONY EVANS

30 Days to Overcoming Addictive Behavior
What if, in the next month, you could break the hold a bad habit has on you? Join Dr. Tony Evans on a 30-day journey filled with powerful biblical insights and practical tips for embracing healing and finding liberation.

30 Days to Overcoming Emotional Strongholds
Dr. Evans identifies the most common and problematic emotional strongholds and demonstrates how you can break free from them—by aligning your thoughts with God's truth in the Bible.

30 Days to Victory Through Forgiveness
Has someone betrayed you? Are you suffering the consequences of your own poor choices? Or do you find yourself asking God, "Why did You let this happen?" Like a skilled physician, Dr. Evans leads you through a step-by-step remedy that will bring healing to that festering wound and get you back on your journey to your personal destiny.

Watch Your Mouth
Your greatest enemy is in your mouth. Dr. Evans reveals life-changing,

biblical insights into the power of the tongue and how your words can be used to bless others or to usher in death. Be challenged to use your mouth to speak life into the world around you. (Also available—*Watch Your Mouth Growth and Study Guide, Watch Your Mouth DVD*, and *Watch Your Mouth Interactive Workbook*.)

Your Comeback

Get inspired by stories of sports teams that won with seemingly no shot at victory, and explore the epic comebacks of biblical heroes with scandalous pasts. You'll be challenged to trust your sovereign Coach with all that lies ahead. (Also available—*Your Comeback DVD* and *Your Comeback Interactive Workbook*.)

A Moment for Your Soul

In this uplifting devotional, Dr. Evans offers a daily reading for Monday through Friday and one for the weekend—all compact, powerful, and designed to reach your deepest need. Each entry includes a relevant Scripture reading for the day. (eBook only)

It's Not Too Late

Dr. Evans uses prominent Bible characters to show that God delights in using imperfect people who have failed, sinned, or just plain blown it. You'll be encouraged as you come to understand that God has you too on a path to success despite your imperfections and mistakes.

The Power of God's Names

Dr. Evans shows that God's nature is revealed through His names. Discover how to know God by His names and experience His love, faithfulness, and power in a deeper way. As you do, you will be better equipped to face the challenges life throws at you.

Praying Through the Names of God

Dr. Evans reveals insights into some of God's powerful names and provides prayers based on those names. Your prayer life will be revitalized as you connect your needs with the relevant characteristics of His names.

Experience the Power of God's Names

Transform your daily life as you learn about the many names of God and the powerful promises they contain. With 85 beautifully designed devotions, this colorful book makes an ideal gift or a great addition to your own quiet time with God.

Victory in Spiritual Warfare

Dr. Evans demystifies spiritual warfare and empowers you with a life-changing truth: Every struggle faced in the physical realm has its root in the spiritual realm. With passion and practicality, Dr. Evans shows you how to live a transformed life in and through the power of Christ's victory.

Prayers for Victory in Spiritual Warfare

Feel defeated? God has given you powerful weapons to help you withstand the onslaught of Satan's lies. This book of prayers, based on Dr. Evans's life-changing book *Victory in Spiritual Warfare*, will help you stand against the enemy's attacks.

Horizontal Jesus

Do you want to sense God's encouragement, comfort, and love for you every day? Dr. Tony Evans reveals that as you live like a horizontal Jesus—giving these things away to others—you will personally experience them with God like never before. (Also available—*Horizontal Jesus Study Guide*.)

To learn more about Harvest House books and
to read sample chapters, visit our website:

www.harvesthousepublishers.com

HARVEST HOUSE PUBLISHERS
EUGENE, OREGON